COMFORT
FOOD

COMFORT FOOD

102
Simple, Hearty, Feel-Good Traditional Recipes to Feed the Body and Nourish the Soul

SUE KREITZMAN

GRAMERCY BOOKS
New York

Copyright © 1986 by Sue Kreitzman.
All rights reserved under International and Pan-American
Copyright Conventions.

This edition is published by Gramercy Books™,
an imprint of Random House Value Publishing, Inc.,
201 East 50th Street, New York, New York 10022.

Gramercy Books™ and design are trademarks of
Random House Value Publishing, Inc.

Random House
New York • Toronto • London • Sydney • Auckland
http://www.randomhouse.com/

Printed and bound in the United States of America

Library of Congress Cataloging-in-Publication Data
Kreitzman, Sue.
    Comfort food: 102 simple, hearty, feel-good traditional recipes
    to feed the body and nourish the soul / by Sue Kreitzman.
        p.   cm.
    Originally published: New York: Harmony Books, 1986.
    Includes index.
    ISBN 0-517-20277-8
    1. Cookery.   I. Title.
    TX652.K633 1999
    641.5—dc21   98-13051
                                                                      CIP

8 7 6 5 4 3 2 1

Contents

Introduction

Temporary sufferers of broken hearts and shattered dreams can always find comfort in a tranquilizing gastronomic interlude. Most people have their own very idiosyncratic version of food to feel better by. Once while on a late-night radio talk show, I asked my listeners to call in with their secret feasts, the voluptuous, private indulgences that they slap together when all alone and in need of a bit of food therapy. The response was over-whelming—the phones lit up with calls, and remained lit up for hours. Many people began shyly: "I've never told anyone about this before," and then let loose with the most mind-boggling snacks imaginable: dill pickles hollowed out and filled with crunchy peanut butter; grilled cheese sandwiches smothered with maple syrup; ketchup sandwiches; and much more—some of it bizarre, some compelling, and all passionate.

"I have a mad passion for fried oatmeal," said one man, who then instructed me on the best way to age leftover oatmeal so that it becomes properly rubbery and gelatinous, and the correct way to fry it so that it becomes crusty. Another man sautés leftover macaroni, sauce and all, in olive oil until crisp, and eats it, alternating bites with a thick sandwich of Genoa salami on white bread.

Of course, this must be eaten in the correct order to be a true secret feast: first a bite of macaroni, then—while the macaroni is still in the mouth—a bite of sandwich, then a glorious chew of the whole mess. This particular feast demonstrates a vital aspect of secret feasts: The proper ritual behavior—the manner of eating—is very important. For instance, a man who dotes on buttermilk and saltines spread with peanut butter assured me that it works only if the buttermilk is *very* sour and the snack is sipped and nibbled in careful sequence. My teenage son eats slices of individually wrapped American cheese while reading mystery books. He holds a slice under the reading lamp until it begins to soften just so, then unwraps it and slowly eats it, reading all the while. He can polish off a pound of cheese and several chapters this way. A woman sets a banana sandwich and a bowl of chili on the table with gleeful anticipation. She alternates spoonfuls of chili with bites of sandwich until the bowl is clean and the sandwich is gone. Secret feasts are funny, sometimes startling, and often scrumptious. Reading or thinking about them makes one want to raid the refrigerator at once. (A bit of cold mashed potatoes perhaps—or some three-day-old pizza . . .)

But there is more to mood food than odd little secret feasts, compelling as they are. Eating to chase the blues away is one of the most elemental of human activities. Food is much more than a matter of vitamins and minerals. Food is solace, a soothing medicine applied to the inner body. This innocent kind of folk medicine is instinctive and sensible; food nourishes both psychically and physically, and is far less damaging than alcohol, drugs, or tobacco.

There are many kinds of comfort foods. Ice cream, pasta in butter and cream, bland soft custards, and other smooth creamy dishes are reminders of Mother. They don't take us back to the womb but to that period shortly thereafter when we were safely cradled and gently fed. Fragrant, gutsy stews, thick chunky soups, and bubbling gratins make us feel safe, warm, and well protected from the raging elements. Old-fashioned desserts that contain plenty of texture and temperature contrasts help us surrender to sensual pleasure and so forget the stresses of a sometimes cruel world. And chocolate, of course, is for many the most powerful culinary therapy of all. One bite of certain densely chocolaty concoctions and the world brightens, the universe sparkles, and angels sing softly in the distance.

Both secret feasts and comfort foods are very personal things. When the blues strike, some people crave sweetness; some need spicy and sour flavors. Many want dramatic contrasts of sweet/sour, hot/cold, spicy/bland, cruncy/smooth. In the interest of culinary therapy for all, I have compiled a group of super-comforting recipes to suit every taste.

There is crunchy crispness and silken smoothness for the texture fanatics; seductive sweetness for those who depend on dessert; mouth-puckering, tongue-tingling tartness and spiciness for the legions who prefer to seek solace in astringency and fire; and plenty of gorgeously decadent chocolate for the chocoholics in our midst. The collection contains oodles of indulgently buttery, creamy sauces and soups for those who crave richness, but should a depression center on escalating weight and an expanding waistline, there are low-cal comforts too. Cooking these recipes will fill your home with warm and cozy odors, and consuming them will soothe you in the deep, dark recesses of the soul that only good food can reach. Some are meant to be private nibbles; others are best shared with good, loving company. I hope they soothe your feelings as they never fail to soothe mine.

RATINGS

The recipes in this book are meant to ease your way through the trials and tribulations of everyday life. To help you obtain the proper comfort that will meet your particular need of the moment, the recipes have been rated as follows:

✻**Comforting** Good for minor aggravations.

✻✻**Very Comforting** Good for blue funks, collywobbles, and mubblefubbles.

✻✻✻**Ultimate, Universal Comforting Power** Save these big guns for disappointments in love, IRS snafus, and other deep woes.

Basic Comforts

**"Nothing like mashed potatoes
when you're feeling blue. Nothing
like getting into bed with a bowl of
hot mashed potatoes already
loaded with butter, and
methodically adding a thin cold
slice of butter to every forkful."**
NORA EPHRON
Heartburn

THE SCIENCE OF COMFORT

Certain foods have universal comforting power. A bowl of mashed potatoes, a tangle of pasta, a heap of grits: all the starchy, high-carbohydrate foods are almost miraculous in their curative powers. There may be good reason for their magical ability to chase the blues. Recent research suggests that certain foods provide contentment and mood elevation by actually altering the amounts of key brain chemicals, in much the same way as drugs used to treat severe depression. A chemical called serotonin must be present in the brain in proper amounts, or downward mood swings occur. Drugs in use for depression keep serotonin levels high by either retarding the body's removal of serotonin or promoting its buildup. The body makes serotonin from one of the components of dietary proteins: the amino acid tryptophan. Under ordinary circumstances, tryptophan has to compete with other amino acids to get into the brain. But when an individual ingests relatively more carbohydrate than protein, tryptophan has less competition getting in. When more tryptophan gets into the brain, more serotonin can be produced, and the individual feels calm and sleepy and much less anxious.

MASHED POTATOES ✖✖✖

There is nothing quite so comforting as a steaming, fluffy mountain of mashed potatoes. The potatoes are wonderful, of course, with a stew or a pot roast that has plenty of rich gravy, but they are even better, at the end of a long hard day, all alone. Just you, a nice big soup spoon, and a warm bowl of mashed potatoes. There's a certain amount of leeway involved in the production of the perfect mountain, but don't fool around with the potato itself. Choose Idaho bakers every time. They are floury, and mash up into a lovely, ethereal cloud. Waxy boiling potatoes, when mashed, produce a sticky mass that gives no comfort whatsoever.

Boil your Idahos, in a covered pot of salted water to generously cover, until tender but not falling apart. For the absolutely best results, boil the potatoes whole and unpeeled; but if you are in a hurry, you can peel and quarter them before boiling, and still end up with a very decent bowl of comfort.

When the potatoes are tender, drain in a colander. If whole and unpeeled, grasp them with an oven mitt, to avoid burns, and scrape off the skins with a table knife. Quarter the potatoes and return them to the pot. If already peeled and quartered, return them to the pot directly after draining.

Cover the pot and shake it over low heat to toss the potatoes as they dry. If you want exceptionally fluffy, airy mashed potatoes, force the potatoes through a ricer into a warm bowl. If you want your potatoes to be a bit denser, with just a hint of a lump here and there, use a potato masher, and mash them right in the pan over *low* heat. Work the potatoes well with the masher. The merest hint of a lump in a bowl of mashed potatoes can be incredibly homey and soothing, but that hint must *never* become actual wholesale lumpiness, or all the medicine is immediately canceled. Mash with vigor and dedication. Never use a food processor to make mashed potatoes; you'll end up with a gluey mess.

When the potatoes are mashed or riced, salt and pepper them. Take a wooden spoon

and beat in some softened butter and some warmed cream, half-and-half, or milk, or room-temperature sour cream. How much is up to you, but this is best when creamy and luxurious. For a change, try beating in chopped onions that have been sautéed to caramelized melting tenderness in plenty of butter and a dab of vegetable oil. When the potatoes are as rich, creamy, and irresistible as you could possibly want, scrape them into a warm bowl, grab a soup spoon, seat yourself in a comfortable chair, and eat blissfully.

BAKED POTATOES ✹✹ They lack the gossamer, ethereal quality of mashed potatoes, but in their own earthy way, baked potatoes are comforting, sustaining, and deeply satisfying. To bake the perfect potato, choose a large unblemished Idaho, scrub it, pierce it in several places with a fork or a thin skewer, and leave it in a 425°F oven for about 1¼ hours. Remove it, perforate it lengthwise and breadthwise with the tines of a fork, and squeeze it so that the tender potato flesh comes surging up. Sprinkle on a bit of salt, grind on some pepper, and you have one of the earth's great foods at its simplest. The nice thing about a baked potato as comfort is that it is a caloric bargain. Should you wish to go beyond the salt-and-pepper embellishment and still keep the calories low, try a squeeze of lemon juice (lemon and potato is a marvelous combination), a scattering of fresh herbs, a dollop of yogurt, a scoop of chèvre, a splash of buttermilk, a shower of grated Parmesan, a deluge of salsa, or a dab or so of good mustard. Of course, if calories are no object, pile on the butter, heavy cream or

sour cream, and shredded cheese and revel in it. Whatever you do, don't neglect to eat the skin. The contrast of crunchy skin against tender flesh is part of what makes a baked potato so special.

"Roasted ... very hot potatoes with salt and fresh butter in them were fit for a woodland king—besides being deliciously satisfying."
FRANCES HODGSON BURNETT
The Secret Garden

PASTA ✹✹✹ Semantically speaking, spaghetti, macaroni, and noodles have vanished from the face of the earth. They are now called by their generic name—pasta—and anyone gauche enough to use the old-fashioned nomenclature is hopelessly out of date. But whatever the semantics, the soothing properties of this well-loved farinaceous food are legendary. For times of emotional emergency, involving perhaps a recalcitrant lover or the Internal Revenue Service, boil a quantity of linguine or spaghetti to the *al dente* stage, drain, and toss with any of a variety of simple, quickly made sauces. All of these suggestions will sauce ¾ to 1 pound of pasta and are adjustable to your needs.
Lemon Cream: Boil 1½ cups heavy cream with the grated rind of ½ lemon. When reduced to approximately 1 cup, remove from the heat, squeeze in the juice of ½ lemon, and season with salt and freshly ground pepper.
Parmesan Cream: Melt ¼ pound butter in 1 cup heavy cream. Simmer together for a few minutes. Stir in 1 cup grated Parmesan

11

cheese. Stir until melted, smooth, and hot. Season with freshly ground pepper if desired. (For an interesting change, substitute Gorgonzola for the Parmesan.)

New Orleans "Shallot" Sauce: Melt ¼ pound butter and let cook over low heat for a few minutes so that it takes on a faintly nutty taste. Do not let it brown. Stir in 1 cup thinly sliced scallions (the white and part of the green) and about ¼ cup chopped fresh parsley. Stir until heated through, but do not let the scallions brown or even get limp. Toss at once with the hot pasta. (This is my version of an utterly simple, fresh-tasting pasta dish served at New Orleans's Pascale's Manale. In New Orleans scallions are called shallots.)

Spicy Cold Tomatoes: This is my personal summer secret feast. My mouth waters just writing about it. Peel, seed, and juice at least 8 (more wouldn't hurt) large, ripe summer tomatoes. Cut them into coarse chunks. Immediately dump them onto the steaming-hot, freshly cooked pasta. Top with about ½ cup cold salsa (Hot Cha-Cha and Enrico are both excellent brands, if you don't have a secret recipe of your own) and eat *at once*. There are no collywobbles in the world that can withstand this one—I love it!

GRITS When properly seasoned and steaming-hot, grits are incredibly soul-satisfying—all alone or as a foil for a variety of gravies, fried fish, eggs (especially poached), or country ham. Served any way at all, grits are pure good eating.

I learned about grits when I moved South sixteen years ago, and they have been an essential part of my home cooking ever since. They come in three forms: regular, quick-cooking, and instant. Instant grits—stirred up right in the bowl with boiling water—are ready in a jiffy with virtually no trouble, but their flavor and texture leave something to be desired. To the grits connoisseur, the quick-cooking variety (5 to 10 minutes cooking time) and the regular variety (which cook for half an hour) are the most satisfying.

The texture is never perfectly smooth because grits are a collection of tiny particles of ground corn hominy. At their most basic, grits are cooked in salted water, peppered (*never* sugared!), buttered, and served piping-hot—usually for breakfast. (The exact cooking time and measurements are on the back of the box.) The salt and pepper are important; without them, the grits are insipid and worthy of Yankee scorn. For an exquisite dish of grits, stir in a generous tot of buttermilk before serving. And to elevate grits to the level of ambrosia, fold in a handful of grated sharp cheddar cheese. When cooking boiled grits for dinner (the perfect complement to roasted meat or poultry with rich gravy), substitute chicken stock for water, and add a few spoonfuls of Parmesan cheese at the end.

If you have leftover grits in the refrigerator, you have several deeply comforting options. Cold grits can be cut into strips, dipped in beaten egg, fried in butter until crisp, and served with maple syrup. Or try baking grits mixed with cheese and eggs. Even better, mash cold grits and spoon dollops into hot oil. Cook these patties as you would potato pancakes, until golden brown and crusty.

Soups

"One small serving of a ravishing soup is infuriating. It is like seeing the Pearly Gates swing shut in one's face after one brief glimpse of heaven."

MARJORIE KINNAN RAWLINGS
Cross Creek Cookery

CHICKEN SOUP

✶✶✶ It really does work. Steaming hot, golden, rich chicken soup calms jittery nerves, soothes jangled pyches, and even helps alleviate some of the peskier symptoms of colds and flu. While you inhale the aromatic steam, and slowly spoon up the chicken broth, you feel beautifully warm, loved, and cared for.

Makes 10 cups

1 (3-pound) chicken with giblets (excluding liver)
Any chicken parts you have saved
3 celery stalks
2 carrots
2 parsnips
1 garlic clove, peeled and lightly crushed
2 thin onion slices
⅓ medium boiling potato, peeled
Salt
Freshly ground pepper (use white pepper if you hate black specks in your soup)
Fresh dill

1. Cut the chicken into parts. Clean well: remove pinfeathers and impurities, pull off excess fat, and rinse in warm water. Scrub the celery, carrots, and parsnips, leaving the carrots and parsnips unpeeled. Cut the vegetables into bite-size pieces.

2. Boil the chicken, giblets, and any extra chicken parts in 1 gallon water. After 10 minutes, skim all foam and scum from top. Add the garlic, vegetables, and a little bit of salt (not too much now, or as the soup cooks down it will become much too salty). Reduce the heat so the liquid stays at a steady simmer. Simmer, partially covered, for 1 hour and 10 minutes.

3. Season with salt and pepper to taste. Allow to cool, partially covered. Strain the soup through a fine sieve. Press down on the solids to extract all their goodness. Pour the soup into jars, cover tightly, and refrigerate.

4. Next day, scrape off the fat. The soup will probably have jelled, a sign that you have made a good, gelatin-rich broth. It will liquefy again when heated. Heat. Stir in dill, taste, and adjust the seasonings. Serve piping-hot.

VEGETABLE SOUP

✲✲ The soothing gentle bubbling of simmering vegetable soup, its heady aroma, and comforting nourishment make it a staple on everyone's list of therapeutic foods. This southern-style vegetable soup is a hearty concoction, so thick that it is almost a stew. Served with cornbread or a loaf of crisp French bread, it is a complete meal.

Serves 8

3 tablespoons bacon fat or vegetable oil
2 large onions, cut in half and sliced into thin half moons
3 large garlic cloves, crushed
3 large carrots, peeled and thickly sliced
1 white turnip, peeled and diced
½ cup trimmed, thickly sliced pole beans
1 can (1 pound 12 ounces) plum tomatoes, undrained and mashed with the hands
6 cups chicken stock
½ teaspoon dried oregano, crumbled
½ teaspoon dried basil, crumbled
1 bay leaf
4 pieces meaty smoked ham hock
2 10-ounce packages frozen chopped greens (turnip or collard are best, but spinach can be substituted), defrosted
½ cup small elbow macaroni

1 can (1 pound) blackeyed peas, well-drained and rinsed (chickpeas or kidney beans can be substituted)
Several dashes of Tabasco sauce
Salt and freshly ground pepper to taste
½ cup fresh chopped parsley

1. Heat the fat or oil in a deep, heavy pot that can be covered. Gently cook the onion and garlic in the fat until soft but not browned.

2. Add the carrots, turnips, and pole beans. Toss them with the onion and garlic. Cook gently for 2 or 3 minutes, stirring occasionally.

3. Stir in the tomatoes, stock, oregano, basil, bay leaf, and ham hocks. Bring to a boil, then partially cover, reduce heat, and simmer gently for 1½ to 2 hours, until everything is tender.

4. Remove the ham hocks and cut the meat off the bones in small chunks. Return the meat to the pot. Discard the fat, bones, and rind.

5. Stir in the greens, macaroni, and blackeyed peas. Simmer an additional ½ hour, or more, until the greens are tender and the macaroni is cooked. Add Tabasco, salt, and pepper to taste. Stir in parsley. This may be served at once, or cooled and refrigerated and served a day or two later. It improves with age. Thin with additional stock if necessary.

OYSTER STEW

✖✖ Oyster stew is powerful medicine. Eat it slowly, letting its subtle flavors curl around your tongue, and the plump, tender oysters slide down slowly and seductively. A steaming bowlful of this magical brew in the evening will surely guarantee sound sleep and pleasant dreams.

Serves 2–4

3 tablespoons butter
5 scallions, trimmed and thinly sliced
1 pint shucked oysters with liquor
Freshly ground black pepper to taste
¼ teaspoon paprika
½ teaspoon Worcestershire sauce
2 cups half-and-half
Salt to taste
1–2 tablespoons softened butter
Cayenne pepper

1. Melt the 3 tablespoons butter in a saucepan. Sauté the scallions until limp but not browned.

2. Set a strainer over a bowl. Dump in the oysters and their liquor. Drain very well and pour the liquor into the saucepan, leaving the oysters in the strainer over the bowl. Add black pepper, paprika, and Worcestershire sauce to the saucepan. Simmer for 5 minutes.

3. Stir in the half-and-half and any additional liquor that has drained from the oysters. Bring to a boil.

4. Stir in the oysters. Immediately turn down the heat to a very gentle simmer. Simmer just until the edges of the oysters ruffle—5 minutes or so, depending on the size of the oysters. Taste, and add a touch of salt if needed.

5. Ladle the stew into heated bowls, dividing the oysters evenly. Float ½ tablespoon softened butter on each serving, and sprinkle with a dusting of cayenne pepper. Serve at once.

"When the cold winds begin to harp and whinny... you will be glad to resume your acquaintance with a bowl of steaming bivalves, swimming in milk, with little clots of yellow butter twirling on the surface of the broth. An oyster stew... will keep your blue eyes blue to any weather."
CHRISTOPHER MORLEY
Travels in Philadelphia

RED BELL PEPPER SOUP

✵✵ Because red bell peppers are very chic, they are available in large numbers in the produce departments of many supermarkets. I'm glad, because I love their fleshy sweetness and brilliant color. They lend both to this gentle soup.

Makes 9 cups

3 tablespoons butter
1 large onion, chopped
8 large red bell peppers, cored, seeded, and
    cut into coarse chunks
5 cups chicken stock
Salt and freshly ground pepper to taste
¼ teaspoon dried thyme
1 cup half-and-half

1. Melt the butter. Sauté the onion until tender but not browned.

2. Add the peppers and toss to coat with butter. Stir in the stock and the seasonings. Simmer, uncovered, for 20 to 30 minutes, until the peppers are very tender. Don't overcook them, or the skin will start to come off and the texture of the soup will be wrong.

3. Let the soup cool and pour it into the container of a food processor. (You will have to do this in several batches.) Pulse the machine on and off two or three times so that the soup is chunky but not puréed. At this point the soup may be refrigerated for several days.

4. At serving time pour the soup into a pot, stir in the half-and-half, and heat. Taste and adjust seasonings.

POTAGE TOASTED FARINA

✽ This porridgelike Swiss soup is good for hangovers, disappointments in love, and general malaise. For best results you really must use a good homemade chicken stock. Without red wine, it is quintessential nursery food; with the wine, an ambrosial adult tonic.

Serves 4

2 tablespoons butter
¾ cup farina (Cream of Wheat)
1 tablespoon flour
1 tablespoon minced onion
6 cups hot chicken stock
¼ cup dry red wine (optional)
Salt and freshly ground pepper to taste

17

1. Melt the butter in a heavy pot. Stir in the farina. Cook, stirring, over low heat until brown and toasted.

2. Whisk in the flour and onion. Cook, stirring, on low heat for 1 minute.

3. Whisk in the hot chicken stock. Simmer for 45 minutes, stirring occasionally. Stir in the red wine and salt and pepper. Simmer for another minute or so and serve.

FONTINA SOUP

✹✹ This recipe was inspired by fonduta—Italian fontina cheese fondue. Should you be lucky enough to have a white truffle on hand, shave it over the soup. But even without the truffle refinement, fontina soup is deliciously restorative.

Serves 4

4 tablespoons butter
1 large onion, finely chopped
4 tablespoons flour
5 cups milk, scalded
Salt
2 cups grated Italian fontina cheese (do *not* substitute Swedish or Danish fontina)
4 thick slices French bread, dried in a low oven and buttered

1. Melt the butter in a heavy pot. Stir in the onion, cover, and steam over low heat for 10 minutes. Uncover, raise the heat a bit, and cook, stirring occasionally, until the onions are very tender but not browned.

2. Turn the heat to low. With a wire whisk, stir in the flour. Whisk for 3 to 4 minutes, until the flour has lost its raw taste. Whisk in the hot milk and bring to a boil. Lower the heat and simmer gently for 10 minutes, stirring occasionally. Lightly season with salt, remembering that the cheese will add more.

3. Remove the soup from the heat. Gently fold in the fontina cheese. Taste, and add more salt if necessary.

4. Place a slice of bread in each of four heated soup bowls. Pour in the soup. Serve at once.

LENTIL SOUP

✹✹ A robust bowl of lentil soup does wonders when the winter blues set in. It will keep for several days in the refrigerator, several months in the freezer. (Dilute the soup with a bit of stock before reheating.) As a change from croutons, garnish the soup with a dollop of sour cream or slices of knockwurst.

Makes 8 cups

1 tablespoon butter
4 slices bacon, cut into 1-inch pieces
3 carrots, peeled and coarsely chopped
2 onions, coarsely chopped
1 stalk celery, coarsely chopped
3 garlic cloves, crushed
1½ cups lentils, rinsed and picked over
8 cups chicken stock
½ pound smoked ham hocks
Salt and freshly ground pepper to taste
1 bay leaf
½ teaspoon dried basil
½ teaspoon dried thyme
½ teaspoon dried oregano
½ cup chopped fresh parsley
Garlic Croutons (recipe follows)

1. Heat the butter and bacon in a heavy soup pot. When the butter is melted, toss in the carrots, onions, celery, and garlic. Cover and steam over low heat for 10 minutes. Uncover, raise the heat a bit, and cook until the vegetables are very tender but not browned.

2. Stir in the lentils, stock, and ham hocks. Bring to a boil. Skim off all foam and scum.

3. Stir in the salt and pepper, bay leaf, basil, thyme, oregano, and parsley. Partially cover the pot and simmer for 40 to 50 minutes, until the lentils are tender. Let cool.

4. Remove the ham hocks and reserve. Fish out the bay leaf and discard. In the container of a food processor, process half the soup to a rough purée by flicking the motor on and off a few times. Combine the puréed and unpuréed soup. Discard the rind, bone, and fat from the ham hocks; dice the meat and return it to the soup. Serve the soup with garlic croutons.

Garlic Croutons
4 slices stale rye bread
1 garlic clove, split

1. Preheat the oven to 250°F.

2. Trim crusts from the bread. Rub the bread with the cut sides of the garlic.

3. Put a rack on a baking sheet. Arrange the bread on the rack and bake for ½ hour, or until browned and crisp. Cube the bread.

BEAN SOUP

✴✴ No one can eat bean soup, especially this Southwestern version, and remain glum. Served with a salad and some guacamole, it's a meal.

Makes 8 cups

¼ pound bacon, diced
1 onion, chopped
1 garlic clove, crushed
1 tablespoon chili powder
½ teaspoon ground cumin
1 pound dried baby lima beans
¼ pound smoked ham hocks
2 quarts water
1 can (1 pound 12 ounces) plum tomatoes,
    drained and crushed
3 tablespoons brown sugar
1 chorizo sausage, sliced into ¼-inch pieces
    (substitute kielbasa if chorizos are un-
    available)
Salt and freshly ground pepper to taste

1. Combine the bacon, onion, and garlic in a deep heavy pot. Cook gently until the onion and garlic are tender but not at all browned.

2. Add the chili powder and cumin. Stir over very low heat until the onion is coated with spices.

3. Add the beans, ham hocks, and water. Bring to a boil, skimming off foam and scum as they rise. Reduce the heat and simmer, partially covered, for 1 ½ hours, or until the beans are just tender.

4. Stir in the tomatoes, brown sugar, chorizo, and salt and pepper. Simmer for approximately 1 hour more, or until the beans are very tender.

5. Fish out the ham hocks. Discard the fat, rind, and bones; cube the meat and return it to the soup. Serve as is or with dollops of sour cream. This soup tastes best on the second day, but it will need to be thinned with stock or water.

"...I awoke at 6:30 A.M. and looked out on a gray landscape that would have dispirited Gustave Doré: palpably damp, lunar in its defoliated desolation, it made my bone marrow feel as though I somehow had extracted it and left it in a dish on the back step all night. It was one of those mornings when a man could face the day only after warming himself with a mug of black coffee beaded with steam, a good thick crust of bread, and a bowl of bean soup."
RICHARD GEHMAN
The Haphazard Gourmet

CARAWAY SOUP

✷✷ I have a passion for Hungarian food. It is the most sensuous, subtle, and rich cuisine I know. Perhaps the fact that I discovered it on my honeymoon influences my strong feelings, but it never fails to delight me. This soup, for instance, with its whisper of caraway, and smooth creaminess offset by crunchy croutons, will send *frissons* of pleasure up and down your spine.

Serves 2

1 tablespoon butter
1 tablespoon flour
1 ½ teaspoons caraway seeds
4 cups hot chicken stock
Salt and freshly ground pepper to taste
1 cup half-and-half
Croutons (recipe follows)

1. Melt the butter in a heavy pot. Whisk in the flour and caraway seeds. Stir over low heat for 3 to 4 minutes.

2. Whisk in the hot stock. Simmer, partially covered, stirring occasionally, for 15 to 20 minutes. Season to taste.

3. Strain the soup and return it to the pot. Stir in the half-and-half. Adjust the seasonings and heat through. Serve piping-hot, with croutons.

Croutons

2 tablespoons butter
1 slice stale rye bread

1. Heat the butter in a small skillet.

2. Trim the crusts from the rye bread. Cube the bread. Toss the cubes in the butter until browned and toasty.

POTATO SORREL SOUP

❋❋ With great enthusiasm, my friend Jep Morgan, an herb farmer, throws handfuls of fresh herbs into his everyday cooking. "This is a two-fisted, stick-to-the-ribs soup," he told me. It is his own creation, and he inevitably whips up a batch when he needs cheering. If you can't find sorrel, substitute fresh spinach leaves and a squeeze of lemon.

Makes 5½–6 cups

½ pound Italian sausage, removed from casings
1 large onion, finely chopped
1 garlic clove, coarsely chopped
4 large Idaho potatoes, peeled and cubed
2 medium carrots, peeled and coarsely chopped
3 cups chicken stock
1 cup chopped parsley
2¼ cups sorrel, stemmed, trimmed of tough center vein, and finely shredded
Salt and freshly ground pepper to taste
¼ cup chopped chives

1. In a heavy pot, cook the sausage with the onion and garlic. Break up the sausage meat with a wooden spoon as it cooks. Drain well in a colander and return it to the pot.

2. Stir in the potatoes, carrots, and stock. Simmer, covered, for 10 to 15 minutes, until the vegetables are tender. With a potato masher, roughly crush the vegetables in the pot.

3. Stir in the parsley, 2 cups sorrel, and the salt and pepper. Simmer very slowly, uncovered, for 5 to 10 minutes. Serve piping-hot. Garnish each serving with chopped chives and shredded sorrel.

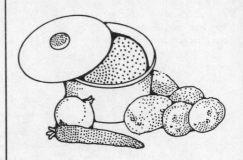

Nibbles and Snacks

"...A little dish of something can spread balm on a wounded psyche, restore balance where there was despondency, the way a gentle spring rain makes a dusty world sparkle again."

NIKA HAZELTON
I Cook As I Please

WRAPPED BRIE WITH CHUNKY TOMATO SAUCE

✗✗ Melted cheese is one of the best medicines for a blue funk—the gooier and runnier the better. A small round Brie, when baked, becomes the runniest, gooiest mood medicine imaginable. When the pastry crust is shattered with a fork, the cheese flows out to mingle with the chunky sauce in a most compelling way. The combination of flavors and textures is very good for the soul.

Serves 2

1 frozen patty shell, thawed
1 8-ounce Brie (underripe), chilled
Chunky Tomato Sauce (recipe follows)

1. Flatten the patty shell with a rolling pin and roll out until large enough to completely enclose the cheese.

2. Wrap the cheese with the pastry, tucking the ends in neatly underneath. Leave no chinks. Return the wrapped cheese to the refrigerator to chill for at least 1 hour.

3. Preheat the oven to 350°F.

4. Place the chilled wrapped cheese in a greased small, shallow baking dish. Bake for 15 minutes, until nicely browned.

5. Spoon the hot tomato sauce onto a warm serving plate. Place the baked cheese on the sauce. If any melted cheese has escaped from the wrapping, quickly pour it over the sauce in a circle around the cheese. Serve at once.

Chunky Tomato Sauce

1 tablespoon olive oil
1 medium onion, coarsely chopped
2 crushed garlic cloves
1 can (1 pound 12 ounces) tomatoes, drained
    and chopped
½ tablespoon chopped fresh basil
1 tablespoon chopped fresh parsley
1 small bay leaf
Salt and freshly ground pepper to taste
1 tablespoon raisins
2 tablespoons pine nuts

1. Heat olive oil in a heavy skillet. Sauté the onion and garlic until tender but not browned. Stir in the remaining ingredients.

2. Simmer for 15 minutes, until the sauce is thick and chunky. Taste and adjust seasonings. Discard the bay leaf.

**"No poem we shall ever see is
Quite as lovely as a Brie is..."**
WILLIAM COLE

24

BRIE BUTTER

Brie, mixed half and half with butter, has a gentle pungency. Brie butter is wonderful spread on thin, crisp toast. Or spread it on rye bread and layer on some ham to make a celestial sandwich.

Makes ½ pound

6–7 ounces ripe Brie
8 tablespoons (1 stick) butter, softened
1 tablespoon chopped chives

1. Remove the rind from the Brie.

2. Put the Brie, butter, and chives in the bowl of a food processor or of an electric mixer fitted with a paddle attachment. Process or beat until thoroughly blended. Store in the refrigerator. Leave out to soften before using.

"Nothing is too good for toast. It deserves the very best we can lavish on it. It is crisp, it is warm, it is buttery, it is faithful...."
VLADIMIR ESTRAGON
Waiting for Dessert

APRICOT JAM

Voluptuous little tongue-teasing lumps of fruit show up here and there in the mass of velvety jam. This Eastern European recipe is marvelous spread generously on a toasted bagel smeared with sweet butter or cream cheese.

Makes 3 cups

1 pound dried apricots
½ – ¾ cup sugar
3–4 tablespoons Cognac

1. Put the apricots in a heavy saucepan. Add water to cover. Bring to a simmer.

2. Cook over low heat, stirring frequently, for about 15 minutes, until the apricots lose their shape and cook into a jamlike mass.

3. Stir in the sugar and Cognac to taste. Cook, stirring, over low heat for a few moments until the sugar is thoroughly dissolved and the mixture is very thick. Be careful not to scorch. Let cool.

4. Scrape the jam into a crock or a bowl. Cover with plastic wrap and refrigerate. It will keep for weeks.

25

WHITE BEAN SPREAD

✹This soothing dip fills the mouth with a delightfully herby, garlicky smoothness. People have been known to attack it with a spoon, and damn the dippers. Don't serve it chilled, or all the good flavor will be muted.

2 cans (15 ounces each) cannellini beans
4 tablespoons olive oil
2 tablespoons wine vinegar
2 tablespoons chopped fresh parsley
2 tablespoons chopped fresh basil
2 large garlic cloves, crushed
Salt
Chopped parsley for garnish
Greek black olives for garnish

1. Put all the ingredients except the garnishes in the work bowl of a food processor fitted with the steel blade. Process until smooth. Taste and add more salt if you feel that it needs it. Scrape the mixture into a bowl. Let mellow for 1 day in the refrigerator.

2. Before serving, bring to room temperature. Sprinkle the surface of the spread with parsley. Slice the olive flesh off the pits and sprinkle the slices around the perimeter of the spread. Serve with crackers or toasted pita bread triangles.

OLIVE SALAD

❧As this mellows in the refrigerator, the flavors blend, and the salad becomes a gloriously oily, fragrant mélange. Keep a spoon near the refrigerator for dipping into the jar at odd moments, or use the mixture to make one of the great sandwiches of all time, the muffuletta (see page 31).

Makes 1 quart

3 cups sliced olives (see note)
1 jar (7 ounces) roasted red peppers, coarsely chopped
2 tablespoons drained capers
½ cup chopped fresh parsley
¼ cup chopped fresh basil
2 garlic cloves, crushed
3 tablespoons red wine vinegar
6 tablespoons olive oil

Toss all the ingredients together in a large bowl. Store in a covered glass jar in the refrigerator. The longer this sits, the better it gets.

NOTE The success of this salad depends on the quality of the olives. Do *not* use canned California olives. Search your local gourmet shops for the best imported olives you can find. There are several excellent Greek brands readily available in jars. One cup of olives should be green, the rest two different varieties of black. With a sharp knife slice the olive flesh off the pits into the measuring cup.

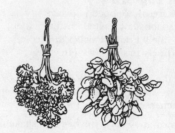

FLAVORED POPCORN

I find plain popcorn (no salt, no fat), popped in an air popper, wonderful comfort food, especially when I'm dieting and ready to sell my soul for something to chew. Dieters can eat handfuls of the crunchy stuff for a very small caloric price. But when calories are no object, there are sinfully caloric things that you can do to popcorn to turn it into a spectacular nibble.

Makes 12 cups

Cheese Popcorn ✷✷

12 cups freshly popped popcorn
8 tablespoons hot melted butter (1 stick)
¼ cup finely grated Parmesan cheese
¼ cup finely grated Gruyère cheese

1. Put the popcorn in a double brown grocery bag. Pour in the hot butter. Dump in the grated cheeses.

2. Immediately close the bag and shake it like mad. Pour the popcorn into a bowl. Serve at once.

Chocolate Popcorn ✷✷✷

2 heaping tablespoons unsweetened cocoa
1–2 level tablespoons confectioners' sugar
12 cups freshly popped popcorn
8 tablespoons hot melted butter (1 stick)

1. Sift the cocoa and sugar together.

2. Put the popcorn in a double brown grocery bag. Pour in the hot butter. Dump in the cocoa mixture.

3. Immediately close the bag and shake it like mad. Pour the popcorn into a bowl. If you can, hide the chocolate popcorn for about 20 minutes before serving so that it can dry a bit. Otherwise, have plenty of paper napkins handy, or else you will be wiping smudgy brown fingerprints off the walls for days.

VARIATIONS Use your imagination to create other flavored popcorns using 12 cups popcorn, 8 tablespoons melted butter, and a doubled paper bag. Here are some ideas for flavorings to add to the butter:

- Lemon, lime, or orange juice and the grated zest of the fruit.
- Tabasco sauce.
- Crushed garlic cloves, cooked gently in the butter until fragrant but not browned.
- A combination of chopped fresh or crumbled dried herbs, stirred briefly in the butter until fragrant.

Sandwiches
and
Light Meals

"Many a one has been comforted in their sorrow by seeing a good dish come upon the table."

E. S. GASKELL
Cranford

TORTA CUBANA

✖✖ I learned to make the most outrageously overstuffed, gooey, soul-satisfying sandwich in the world in Atlixco, Mexico, at the market. My friends and I stopped to rest our weary feet and to quaff some cold beer at a lunch counter called "Meche Tortas y Tacos." As we drank we watched the owner's niece, Carmen Cervantes, hand out drinks and make sandwiches for the hungry lunch crowd. One sandwich in particular—the torta Cubana—was ordered over and over again. Soon we felt impelled to ask Carmen to make one for us. And another. And another. It was the sandwich experience of a lifetime.

Chorizo sausage, crumbled or diced
Large crusty rolls
Thin slices of ham
Grated cheese (a mixture of Jarlsberg, sharp
　　white cheddar, and Monterey Jack will
　　approximate the Mexican cheeses)
Ripe avocados, split and pit removed
Sliced tomato
White onion, thinly sliced and separated into
　　rings
Sliced pickled jalapeños
Mayonnaise

1. Heat a large heavy skillet. Toss the chorizo in the skillet briefly until it is lightly browned and has rendered some of its fat. Remove the sausage with a slotted spoon and set aside.

2. Cut the rolls in half. Scoop out some of the crumb from the top and bottom half. Place the rolls, cut side down, in the skillet to toast lightly. Set aside.

3. Place slices of ham in the skillet and let cook for a few moments. With tongs, turn the slices over. Cover each slice with a *very generous* handful of grated cheeses. Clap the cover on the skillet, turn off the heat, and let sit for a few minutes until the cheese melts into a glorious, soft, gooey mass.

4. Meanwhile, scoop out some ripe avocado and spread it like butter on the bottom half of each roll. Top with a slice of tomato, some onion, some jalapeños, and some crumbled chorizo. Spread some mayonnaise on the top half of each roll.

5. With a broad spatula, lift each slice of cheese-smothered ham onto the bottom half of the roll. Cover with the mayo-spread top half, press together, and eat at once.

PARTY MUFFULETTA

✻The muffuletta, a large, round sandwich of sliced Italian meats and cheeses smothered with a liberal amount of olive salad, was invented at New Orleans's Central Grocery. Standard procedure in New Orleans is to purchase one of these monsters at the Grocery and then to wander—dripping and munching—over to the railroad tracks, there to contemplate the great complexities of life while gazing at the Mississippi and engulfing every last crumb of sandwich. I have reduced the muffuletta to its vital ingredients: bread, olive salad, and salami. Make this large version to comfort a group of friends, or make a small one for a private feast by scraping the crumb out of a crusty roll, filling it with olive salad and salami slices, and weighting it for an hour or two, wrapped in foil, as described in the recipe.

Makes an 18-inch sandwich; serves approximately 9

1 long loaf crusty French bread (about 18 inches long)
1 quart Olive Salad (page 27)
¼ pound thinly sliced Genoa salami

1. Halve the French bread but do not cut it all the way through, so that it opens on a hinge, like a book. Scoop out some of the crumb from each half, leaving ½-inch-thick shells. (Let the crumb dry out and use it for homemade bread crumbs.) Pack the olive salad and its juices on both halves, dividing it equally.

2. Roll each slice of salami. Arrange the rolls in two rows down half of the sandwich.

3. Bring the two halves together. Wrap the sandwich very tightly in two layers of aluminum foil. Place the sandwich on a flat surface. Put weights down its length—bricks or heavy canned goods. Let rest, weighted, at room temperature for 2 to 3 hours.

4. To serve, remove the weights and unwrap. Put the sandwich on a long cutting board. With a sharp serrated knife, slice off 2-inch portions of sandwich.

HAMBURGERS

✱✱✱ Don't think about the flat, juiceless, gristly meat patties served in so many fast-food joints. A thick, rare, black-crusted hamburger is a great pleasure, especially when jammed into a good crusty roll and blanketed with caramelized onions. When only juicy, meaty comfort will do, I'd much rather have one of these burgers than a hunk of steak. This method of pan-frying hamburgers produces a lot of smoke, so don't attempt it unless you have a powerful exhaust fan.

Serves 4

1 ½ pounds ground chuck (use the freshest meat possible)
Salt and freshly ground pepper to taste
Oil
Caramelized onions (cook according to directions in Step 2 of Onion Bread Pudding, page 35)

1. Sprinkle the ground meat with salt and plenty of pepper. Toss gently with two forks. Divide the ground meat into four portions. Handling the meat as gently as possible, shape each portion into a rough patty. Do not press them down. Each patty will resemble a lumpy meatball.

2. Choose a heavy, well-seasoned cast iron skillet. Film the bottom with a very small amount of oil and heat. Sear the hamburger over high heat for a minute on one side, loosen with a pancake turner, turn gently, and sear for a minute on the second side. Reduce the heat and cook until the meat is done the way you like it. Avoid cooking the hamburgers to the well-done stage, when they become dry, gray, and thoroughly unappetizing.

3. Blot the hamburgers on paper towels and place on crusty rolls. Top each burger with a heap of onions, and pass old-fashioned fries (page 74).

CHEESEBURGERS To make wonderfully cheesy cheeseburgers, add 2 cups grated Swiss cheese to the ground chuck. Combine the meat, salt and pepper, and cheese very gently with your hands. Shape into four fat patties and cook as above.

"When I am in trouble, eating is the only thing that consoles me."
OSCAR WILDE
The Importance of Being Earnest

SECRET SANDWICHES

When people shyly disclose their innermost food secrets, when they reveal their favorite secret feasts, the ones that never let them down, even in times of deepest despair, a sandwich or two inevitably tops the list. There is something about two pieces of bread stuffed with wonderful (and often zany) ingredients that pleases and soothes even the glummest sandwich eater right down to his or her toes. Here is a list of secret sandwiches that I have collected over the years, as people have bared their gastronomic souls to me. These eccentric sandwiches have all at one time or another comforted someone in an hour of need.

Potato chip sandwich: A friend swears by this one. Thickly spread 2 slices of white bread with mayonnaise. Place a generous handful of potato chips on one piece of bread, cover with the second, and press down with your hand until you hear the chips go *crunch!* Eat at once, before the chips can get soggy. Another person has confessed to secret feasting on a variation of this sandwich: the fried potato sandwich. She spreads mayonnaise on her fried potato sandwiches, but ketchup would be a perfectly logical substitution.

Countless people find peanut butter sandwiches, in one form or another, an ultimate secret feast. Never *plain* peanut butter, however. It's the combination of peanut butter with something else that works magic. Some tried-and-true examples: peanut butter and banana (mayonnaise optional), a universally winning combination (cheddar cheese and bacon can be added at your discretion); peanut butter and coleslaw; peanut butter and chocolate chips; or peanut butter (crunchy) and marshmallow cream.

Pita bread spread lavishly with a mixture of mayonnaise, ketchup, and mustard, and stuffed with chopped salami and chopped tomatoes.

Liverwurst and melted cheddar on a cinnamon bun.

Raw mushrooms, alfalfa sprouts, and blue cheese dressing on whole-wheat raisin bread.

Chopped cucumbers folded into mayonnaise, seasoned with an extravagant amount of black pepper, and spread on crackers or toast.

Chopped raw garlic mixed into sour cream and spread on crusty rye.

Cannibal sandwich: very fresh top round, ground twice and mixed with chopped scallions, salt, and pepper, and spread raw on German pumpernickel.

Ham sandwich on rye, with mayonnaise spread on one slice of bread and hot pepper jelly on the other.

Thinly sliced onion on cold biscuits with a side of buttermilk.

Mayonnaise, ripe avocado, and hot mustard on whole-wheat bread.

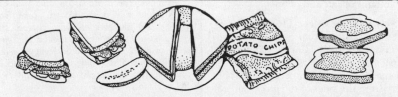

TUNA SPREAD

✹✹ Good old tuna fish sandwiches have comforted myriad individuals through the turmoils of childhood, adolescence, and adulthood. My favorite tuna salad is a dense, spreadable mixture, almost like a tuna pâté, and tastes of good tuna—not extraneous ingredients.

Makes 2 cups

2 cans (7 ounces each) dark tuna, packed in water
½ cup mayonnaise
Juice of 1 lemon
Salt and freshly ground pepper to taste
½ stalk celery
½ small onion

1. Drain the tuna very well. Place in a mixing bowl. With a fork, mash the tuna until it is very fine.

2. Mix in the mayonnaise, lemon juice, and a small amount of salt and pepper.

3. Coarsely chop the celery. Place in a food processor bowl, fitted with the steel blade, and process until finely minced. (This is a very small amount of celery, but it will be minced exactly right in a processor.) Scrape the celery from the sides of the processor bowl and add to the tuna.

4. With a chef's knife, mince the onion very fine. (Don't use the processor for the onion; it will become too watery for this recipe.)

5. Stir the vegetables into the tuna mixture. Scrape into a crock or small bowl and refrigerate until needed. Use for sandwiches or as a great spread on crackers.

TUNA MELT

Much as I love it, my well bred and understated recipe for tuna spread sometimes seems a little too refined. I find myself longing for something gooey, runny and excessive; something *outrageous* although still tuna fish. Such longings demand that juvenile, unsubtle and overbuilt sandwich, the tuna melt.

Make one as follows: Drain a can of tuna fish. Make tuna salad by mashing it up and mixing it with too much Hellman's mayonnaise, an excess of coarsely chopped celery, carrot and onion, and plenty of freshly ground black pepper. A little cayenne is good, too, if you like it. Put the mixture in the freezer for just a few minutes (you want it to be very cold, but not frozen) while you toast a half a bagel or an English muffin. Preheat the broiler.

Remove the tuna from the freezer and thickly pile it on the half bagel or muffin. Top with sliced munster or swiss cheese. Broil it quickly until the cheese is melted and speckled with brown. Remove it and eat *at once*. The cheese is hot and gooey, the tuna salad is cold and creamy, the bread is crisp and crunchy. What a sandwich!

ONION BREAD PUDDING

★★★ This pudding is for people who find comfort in the gobs of melted cheese, the thick crouton, and the dark rich onions that are the glory of onion soup. Onion bread pudding is the soul of onion soup. It is, essentially, onion soup without the soup. Use the largest, sweetest yellow onions that you can find: Bermudas, Vidalias, Walla Walla Sweets, etc.

Serves 6

8 tablespoons (1 stick) butter
1 tablespoon corn oil
8 cups thinly sliced onions
¼ cup dry vermouth
1 large garlic clove, split
6 ounces stale crusty French bread, cut into
    1-inch chunks
2 cups grated Gruyère cheese
3 eggs
2 cups half-and-half
Salt and freshly ground pepper to taste

1. Preheat the oven to 350°F.

2. Melt 4 tablespoons butter with the corn oil in a heavy pot. Toss in the onions, cover, and steam over low heat for 15 minutes. Uncover the pot, raise the heat to medium, and cook, stirring occasionally, until the onions are deeply browned and caramelized. Pour in the vermouth and boil until the liquid cooks away, scraping the bottom of the pot with a wooden spoon all the while.

3. Choose a shallow round 1½-quart gratin dish. Rub it thoroughly with the cut sides of the garlic clove. Discard the garlic.

4. Toss the bread and onions together. Spread them in the gratin dish. Melt the remaining butter and pour it over the bread. Sprinkle on the grated cheese.

5. Beat the eggs lightly and beat in the half-and-half and salt and pepper. Pour the mixture evenly over the bread and cheese. Press the bread into the liquid with a spatula. Let stand for at least an hour. (The gratin may be covered and refrigerated overnight. On the next day bring it to room temperature before proceeding.)

6. Bake for 30 to 40 minutes, until set, puffed, and golden. Serve at once.

"I had never really understood Wolfe's relapses . . . while it lasted . . . he went to bed and stayed there, living on bread and onion soup."
REX STOUT
Fer-De-Lance

RED PEPPER CHEESE PUDDING

✖✖ This delicate, creamy pudding makes a lovely breakfast, or a light meal at any time of day when you want something delicious, simple, and unchallenging. The strips of red pepper peep out of the golden yellow custard in a most attractive manner.

Serves 4–6

2 tablespoons butter
½ tablespoon olive oil
4 red bell peppers, cut into strips about ¾ inch wide
Salt and freshly ground pepper
3 eggs
1 cup cottage cheese
½ cup heavy cream
¼ pound fontina cheese, grated

1. Preheat the oven to 350°F. Butter a 9-inch deep-dish Pyrex pie plate or an 8-inch square 1½-quart Pyrex baking dish.

2. Heat the butter and oil in a skillet. Toss the pepper strips for a minute or so in the oil. Cover the skillet and steam the peppers over low heat for 5 minutes. Uncover and cook gently until the peppers are very tender. Blot the peppers dry on paper towels. Spread the peppers in the buttered dish. Season with salt and pepper.

3. Beat the eggs. Beat in the cottage cheese and cream. Fold in the fontina cheese. Season with salt and pepper to taste. Spread the mixture evenly over the peppers. Bake for 45 minutes, until set and golden. Let cool on a rack for 10 minutes. The pudding is also excellent cold.

CREAMED CHIPPED BEEF

✖✖ Forget everything you have heard about creamed chipped beef, especially nasty nicknames you may have heard from veterans of World War II. This is a luxurious small feast that is perfect for eating alone in sloppy, grumpy privacy, or in the company of one loving and supportive friend or relation.

Serves 2

¼ cup sliced scallions
⅔ cup imported dry vermouth
2 cups heavy cream
Freshly ground pepper to taste
1 jar chipped beef
2 freshly baked potatoes

1. Combine scallions and vermouth in a heavy saucepan. Boil until the liquid is reduced to approximately 1 tablespoon.

2. Stir in the cream. Boil until reduced by approximately ½ cup. Grind in some pepper. (No salt—the chipped beef is salty.)

3. Shred the chipped beef with a sharp knife. Stir it into the sauce. Simmer for 5 minutes.

4. Perforate the potatoes lengthwise and breadthwise with the tines of a fork and pinch them open. Ladle half of the creamed chipped beef over each. Serve at once.

DELI OMELET

✹✹A good deli omelet is made just like an Italian frittata.

Serves 4–6

2 tablespoons oil
1 tablespoon rendered chicken fat (or use all oil)
8 eggs
3 tablespoons water
Salt and freshly ground pepper to taste
1 ½ cups filling (kosher frankfurters or knockwurst, sliced ½ inch thick; quartered ½-inch-thick slices of kosher salami; or very coarsely chopped pastrami or corned beef)
dark mustard

1. Heat oil and fat in a 10-inch nonstick omelet pan.

2. With a fork beat the eggs in a bowl with the water and salt and pepper. (Add salt sparingly; too much will harden the egg protein.) The yolks and whites should be well blended, but do not overbeat. Stir in the filling.

3. Tilt the omelet pan so that it is evenly coated with the hot fat. Pour the egg mixture into the pan. Make sure the filling is evenly distributed throughout the eggs. Cook over medium heat for a minute or two without stirring, so the eggs begin to set on the bottom.

4. With a pancake turner, lift the edge of the omelet away from the pan and tilt the pan so that the uncooked egg flows beneath the cooked portion. Continue doing this all around the pan, until the omelet is almost completely set but still soft and runny in the center.

5. Invert a plate over the omelet pan. Reverse the pan so that the omelet is now on the plate, cooked side up. Carefully slide the omelet back into the pan, uncooked side down. Cook for a few more minutes, so that the bottom is very lightly browned and the eggs are cooked through. (Do not overcook!)

6. Bring to the table in the omelet pan. Divide into equal wedges and serve. Pass the mustard. (Leftover wedges of this omelet are delectable served cold.)

EGGS AND PROSCIUTTO IN FONTINA CREAM

✸Italian fontina cheese, with its low melting point, is a wondrous cooking cheese. Here it melts into reduced cream to form a lavishly rich sauce for boiled eggs and bits of prosciutto.

Serves 6

2 cups heavy cream
Juice of 1 lemon
1 cup grated Italian fontina cheese
¼ pound prosciutto, minced
6 hard-boiled eggs, halved lengthwise

1. Preheat the oven to 350°F.

2. In a deep heavy saucepan, boil the cream until reduced by about half. Stir in the lemon juice.

3. Combine the fontina and prosciutto. Spread half of the mixture on the bottom of a shallow 8-inch square baking dish. Place the eggs on the bed of cheese and ham. Cover with the remaining mixture. Pour and scrape the thickened cream sauce over the whole thing.

4. Cook in the oven for 20 to 30 minutes, until hot and bubbly. Serve at once.

SCRAMBLED EGGS

✸✸✸ This is the simplest and most soothing of dishes. Don't be in a hurry—the secret of successful scrambled eggs is patient stirring over low heat. The crispness of the snow pea garnish nicely sets off the unctuous softness of the eggs, and the brilliant red of the pepper purée is a lovely color contrast to their bright yellow. Pour some of the purée over the eggs, if you wish. Don't be afraid of the roasted garlic. It adds a mild and mysterious dimension to the scrambled eggs; not a strong taste at all. The only beverage to consider having with these eggs is a glass of Champagne.

38

Serves 6

12 eggs, at room temperature
Salt and freshly ground pepper to taste
½ teaspoon dried tarragon
6 tablespoons butter, softened
2 tablespoons finely grated cheese (fontina,
    Parmesan, or Gruyère) (optional)
Pulp from one head of roasted garlic (page
    70)
Chopped fresh parsley
Sautéed Snow Peas (recipe follows)
Scallions on Red Pepper Purée (page 66)
Bacon strips

1. Break the eggs into a large bowl. Add salt and pepper, but go easy on the salt; too much will toughen the egg protein. Crumble the dried tarragon between your fingers and add to the eggs.

2. With a fork, beat the eggs until the whites and yolks are well blended. Do not overbeat.

3. In a heavy, nonstick 9- or 10-inch skillet, melt 4 tablespoons butter. Pour in the eggs and let them spread out in the pan. Keep the heat very low as you stir the eggs constantly and gently from side to side and from top to bottom, with a wooden spoon or spatula. Under no circumstances may the eggs become brown or crusty on the bottom, and lumps must not form.

4. When the eggs become thick and custardy, but are still quite moist, stir in the grated cheese, the remaining softened butter, and the garlic. Stir over low heat until the butter and cheese are melted. Scrape the soft mass

of scrambled eggs onto a warm platter, garnish with parsley, and surround with sautéed snow peas, scallions on red pepper purée, and bacon.

Sautéed Snow Peas
2 tablespoons butter
2 tablespoons corn oil
2 pounds snow peas
Juice of ½ lime
Salt and freshly ground pepper to taste

1. Heat the butter and oil in a heavy, wide skillet or wok.

2. Toss the snow peas in the hot fat. Squeeze in the lime juice. Toss and cook until they are shiny and partially cooked. They must remain very crisp and bright green.

3. Season with salt and pepper. Serve at once.

**"There are times when there is nothing so beautiful, so soul satisfying as bacon and eggs."
Lux Radio Theater production of H. G. Wells's *War of the Worlds***

OVEN PANCAKE

✸✸This is good for breakfast, as a dessert, or anytime you want *something* but are not sure exactly what. It emerges from the oven light and eggy, and not at all sweet. Sugar and lemon juice are added to each portion in whatever quantity is pleasing, just before eating.

Serves 2–4

½ cup flour
½ cup buttermilk
Pinch of salt
2 eggs
4 tablespoons butter
Brown sugar
Lemon wedges

1. Preheat the oven to 425°F.

2. Briefly beat together the flour, buttermilk, salt, and eggs. The batter will be lumpy.

3. Put the butter in a 9-inch deep-dish Pyrex pie plate and place in the oven until the butter is melted and very hot. Pour in the batter. Bake for 15 minutes, until golden and puffed all around the edge. Serve in wedges, sprinkled with brown sugar and a generous squeeze of lemon juice.

PIZZA

There's deep-dish Chicago and flat New York style; round and square; Sicilian and individual pan; plain cheese and everything on it; thick crust and thin. Nouvelle chefs festoon their pizza crusts with an unsettling variety of oddities: duck sausage, crayfish, goat cheese, caviar; but many people are convinced that the basic tomatoey, cheesy style enjoyed during their hungry adolescent years is the only kind worth sinking teeth into. Pizza is great fun to make at home, but sometimes a pizza attack strikes and you've *got* to have one right away.

There are some black moods that can be lightened only by a crusty, gooey, drippy, oily, spicy pizza. Alas, by the time you have mixed and kneaded the dough, given it its two risings, prepared the toppings, and baked it, the mood is blacker, and the kitchen is a mess.

Some people try to solve this problem by constructing fast pseudo-pizzas: canned pizza sauce and grated cheese on English muffins, tomato sauce and sliced mozzarella on pita bread, and so on. These ersatz pies are interesting and even tasty, but *they are not pizza* and therefore have little mood-changing ability. You must, at moments like this, use your phone.

Dotted all over America are neighborhood pizza-delivery services—they have done wonders for the country's morale, and there is very likely one in your neighborhood. Call and order, and when your gorgeous pizza arrives, grab it and take it to bed. If possible, take a congenial and loving companion, too. Double cheese, pepperoni, a warm bed, and thou. It's quite a combination.

Main Dishes

"Each country has dishes and treats that give pleasure, comfort, and lift in time of need. In America, abundance has produced a whole constellation of things to eat and drink for sure gratification and instant solace. The favorites among them not only taste good, but seem to make life smoother."

KAY and MARSHALL LEE
America's Favorites

GRATIN OF HERBED OYSTERS

✱✱I can't think of any other culinary experience that is quite as intense as the consumption of a dish of perfectly cooked oysters. When cooked properly, they swell up with their own juices, and then surrender those hot sweet juices in each mouthful. In this recipe the oysters are baked with fresh herbs and garlic.

Serves 4

4 slices good white bread
1 tablespoon fresh thyme leaves
1 tablespoon fresh oregano leaves
1 tablespoon chopped fresh basil
1 tablespoon chopped fresh parsley
½ teaspoon chopped fresh rosemary leaves
Freshly ground pepper
8 tablespoons (1 stick) butter
¼ cup olive oil
5 large garlic cloves, crushed
Juice of 1 large lemon
¼ teaspoon cayenne pepper
1 cup grated Parmesan cheese
1½ pints oysters, well drained

1. Leave the bread slices to dry out on a rack for several hours.

2. Break the bread into pieces and put in the container of a food processor or a blender.

Add the herbs. Process or blend to make fine crumbs. Pour into a bowl and set aside. You should have about 2 cups of flavored crumbs. Grind in some pepper. Set aside.

3. Preheat the oven to 450°F.

4. In a heavy skillet, heat the butter and olive oil. When the butter is melted, add the garlic. Cook very gently for 5 minutes or so, until very fragrant, but do not allow the garlic to brown. Stir in the lemon juice and cayenne pepper. Cook gently for 5 minutes more.

5. Stir in the bread crumbs and Parmesan cheese. Choose a gratin dish that is of a size to hold the oysters in one layer. Sprinkle half the buttered crumbs on the bottom of the dish. Place the oysters on the crumbs. Cover with the remaining crumbs.

6. Bake for 15 to 18 minutes, until the gratin is well browned and bubbly and the oysters are plumped and heated through. Serve at once.

"A beatific smile spread over his face! Man had tasted the oyster!"
DON MARQUIS
The Revolt of the Oyster

HOT DOG RAGOUT

✗✗Kosher hot dogs make a wonderful stew. Real Hungarian paprika is essential. Many supermarkets carry red cans of the aromatic spice in their gourmet department.

Serves 4–6

3 tablespoons chicken fat or vegetable oil
3 large onions, coarsely chopped
2 cloves garlic, minced
2 large green peppers, coarsely chopped
2 tablespoons Hungarian paprika
1 teaspoon marjoram
Salt and freshly ground black pepper to taste
Pinch or 2 of cayenne pepper, to taste
1 large can (1 pound 12 ounces) tomatoes, drained and crushed with your hands
5–6 medium potatoes, peeled and cut into 1-inch cubes
1–1½ cups chicken stock
1 pound kosher frankfurters, sliced into ½-inch pieces
½ cup diced green pepper
½ cup chopped parsley

1. Heat the fat in a deep heavy pot. Toss in the onions and garlic. Cover the pot and let the onions steam over low heat for 10 minutes. Uncover, raise the heat, and cook the onions until browned. Toss in the green pepper and cook, stirring occasionally, until they are limp.

2. Stir in the paprika, marjoram, salt and black pepper, and cayenne pepper. Stir for a minute or two, until the vegetables are well coated with the spices. Stir in the tomatoes, potatoes, and enough stock to barely cover the contents of the pot. Bring to a boil, reduce the heat, and simmer, covered, until the potatoes are almost done.

3. Stir in the frankfurters and simmer, uncovered, until the potatoes are completely done. Garnish with the diced raw green pepper and chopped parsley just before serving.

43

GRATIN OF RED BEANS AND SAUSAGE

❄Sausages and beans go together like Gilbert and Sullivan, Nero and Archie, or Fred and Ginger. This particular version of the time-honored combination is the kind of unpretentious home cooking that tastes so good at the end of a long and complicated day.

Serves 6

1 ½ tablespoons olive oil
1 ½ tablespoons butter
2 medium onions, coarsely chopped
1 stalk celery, coarsely chopped
1 small bell pepper, coarsely chopped
2 garlic cloves, crushed
½ cup red wine
1 can (1 pound 12 ounces) tomatoes, drained
    and chopped
1 bay leaf
½ teaspoon dried thyme
Salt and freshly ground pepper to taste
1 pound smoked kielbasa, sliced ½ inch thick
2 cans (15 ounces each) red kidney beans,
    drained and rinsed
½ cup bread crumbs
2 tablespoons melted butter

1. Preheat the oven to 400°F.

2. Heat olive oil and butter in a heavy skillet. Toss in the onions, celery, bell pepper, and garlic. Cover and steam over low heat for 10 minutes. Uncover, turn up the heat a bit, and cook gently until the onions are golden and the vegetables are tender.

3. Stir in the wine, tomatoes, and seasonings. Simmer for 10 minutes.

4. Combine the sausage and beans and spread them in a 9 x 13 x 2-inch baking dish. Pour the tomato mixture over the beans, sprinkle with the crumbs, and drizzle with melted butter. Bake, uncovered, for 1 hour. Discard the bay leaf before serving.

"I don't think that there is such a thing as bad chili."
LUDWIG BEMELMANS
McCall's magazine, August, 1959

CHILI

✳✳✳ A bubbling pot of chili, surrounded by bowls of garnishes that provide taste, texture, and temperature contrasts, seems to please even (especially!) the most jaded palates. What a happy escape when one feels surfeited with excessive flights of nouvelle cuisine fancies.

Serves 6

2 tablespoons vegetable oil
3 large onions, coarsely chopped
2 garlic cloves, crushed
4 tablespoons chili powder
1 teaspoon ground cumin
1 teaspoon dried oregano
1 teaspoon red pepper flakes, or as needed
3 pounds well-trimmed pork shoulder
    (Boston butt) cut into ½-inch cubes
1 can (6 ounces) tomato paste
Salt and freshly ground pepper to taste
Chicken stock as needed
Garnishes (see below)

1. Preheat the oven to 350°F.

2. Heat the oil in a stewpot. Toss in the onions, cover, and steam for 10 minutes. Uncover, raise the heat a bit, and cook, stirring occasionally, until the onions are golden brown. Stir in the garlic, chili powder, cumin, oregano, and pepper flakes. (The amount of pepper flakes needed depends on your taste and the strength of the chili powder.) Stir over very low heat until the onions are coated with the spice mixture.

3. Stir in the pork, tomato paste, and salt and pepper. Pour in enough chicken stock to just barely cover the contents. Bake in the oven for 30 minutes.

4. Turn the oven down to 250°F and bake for another 1 to 1½ hours, until the meat is very tender and the sauce is thick and rich. During this time adjust the oven temperature down, if necessary, so that the stew remains at a slow simmer.

5. Serve the chili with Custardy Corn Bread (page 63); cooked kidney beans; sour cream; grated cheddar cheese; ripe avocado mashed with lime juice, salsa, and a touch of sour cream; Scallion Salad (recipe follows); chopped fresh coriander leaves; and chopped raw onion.

Scallion Salad

2 bunches scallions, trimmed and thinly
    sliced
1 cup chopped fresh parsley
4 tablespoons olive oil
1½ tablespoons wine vinegar
Salt and freshly ground pepper to taste

Combine and chill.

WILD RICE STRUDEL

✳✳ No one remains unmoved when faced with this symphony of crisp buttery pastry layers, earthy wild rice, salty feta, rich nuts, and mustardy sauce. It is a creation of Patrick Burke, chef and owner of Patrick's Cafe in Atlanta. Patrick changes his menu every few months, but this is the only recipe that survives the change.

Serves 10

4 tablespoons butter
2 large onions, chopped
½ pound mushrooms, thinly sliced
1 cup raw wild rice, cooked (recipe follows)
2 tablespoons chopped pimientos
4 ounces feta cheese, crumbled
¼ cup shelled pistachios
2 eggs, lightly beaten
½ package strudel or phyllo dough (about 10 sheets), thawed, well wrapped, in the refrigerator overnight
1 cup melted butter (2 sticks)
Bread crumbs
Mustard Cream Sauce (recipe follows)

1. Melt 4 tablespoons butter in a skillet. Toss in the onions, cover, and steam over low heat for 10 minutes. Uncover, raise the heat a bit, and cook until the onions are very tender but not browned.

2. Melt 4 tablespoons of butter in another skillet. Toss in the mushrooms and sauté until the mushrooms are very tender and most of their liquid has cooked away.

3. Combine the onions, mushrooms, wild rice, pimientos, feta cheese, and pistachios. Stir in the eggs. The mixture will probably not need salt because of the feta cheese and wild rice, but taste to make sure.

4. Slightly dampen three dish towels. Place one towel on your work surface. Have the melted butter and a brush nearby.

5. Unwrap the thawed strudel dough. Unroll it and place the stack on the first towel. Cover with the second towel. Place the third towel on your work surface. Remove a sheet of dough from the stack and place it on the third towel. Keep the stack covered. Brush the sheet with melted butter and sprinkle evenly with bread crumbs. Repeat until all the sheets are used. Brush the very top sheet with butter but do not sprinkle it with bread crumbs.

6. Preheat to 400°F.

7. Spoon the wild rice mixture onto the strudel in a strip that begins 2 inches from the long edge of the dough. Turn the margin over onto the filling. Lift the edges of the towel and let the strudel roll over onto itself to enclose the filling and form a cylinder. Pick up the towel with the strudel and place it on a greased baking sheet. Gently pull the towel

from the bottom to release it. Brush the top of the strudel with melted butter.

8. Bake for 30 to 45 minutes, until nicely browned. Allow to stand for 10 minutes. Slice, cover each slice with mustard cream sauce, and serve.

Wild Rice

1 cup wild rice
3 cups water
Salt

1. Put the wild rice in a sieve. Rinse under cold water.

2. Put the wild rice, water, and salt in a deep saucepan. Bring to a boil, uncovered, stirring frequently.

3. Reduce the heat, cover, and simmer, stirring occasionally, for 35 to 45 minutes, until the wild rice is cooked. Some of the grains will open, some will not, but the wild rice should be medium-tender, not very soft. Exact cooking time varies with the wild rice itself.

Mustard Cream Sauce

1 quart heavy cream
1½–2 tablespoons Dijon mustard

Bring the cream to a boil in a deep heavy pot. Boil until reduced by half. Stir in the mustard. Serve warm or at room temperature.

BEEF GOULASH

✖✖ A pot of thick, fragrant stew fills the soul with warmth and joy. If the stew is Hungarian, so much the better. Serve this with noodles tossed with melted butter, poppy seeds, and chopped walnuts.

Serves 6

4 tablespoons bacon fat
5 large onions, coarsely chopped
4 large bell peppers, coarsely chopped
3 garlic cloves
½ teaspoon caraway seeds
2 tablespoons Hungarian paprika

3 pounds well-trimmed stewing beef cut into 1-inch cubes
1 can (6 ounces) tomato paste
Salt and freshly ground pepper to taste
Sour cream

1. Preheat the oven to 350°F.

2. Heat the fat in a heavy pot. Toss in the onions, cover, and cook over low heat for 10 minutes. Uncover, raise the heat a bit, stir in the bell peppers, and cook until the onions are very tender and the peppers are beginning to be tender.

3. Chop together the garlic and caraway seeds. Add them to the pot, along with the

paprika. Cook over very low heat until the vegetables are well coated with the spices and the paprika has lost its raw taste.

4. Stir in the beef. Stir over low heat until the meat has lost its redness. Stir in the tomato paste and the salt and pepper.

5. Bake in the oven, covered, for 30 minutes. Reduce the oven temperature to 250°F and cook for 1 to 1½ hours, until the meat is tender. Adjust the oven temperature if necessary so that the contents of the pot remain at a gentle simmer.

6. Serve in shallow soup bowls with a dollop of sour cream on each portion. This recipe may be made in advance and refrigerated for several days. It improves with age.

"What a nice Sunday! A beef stew simmering in the low-ceilinged, blue-tiled kitchen, the whole house fragrant with the scent of herbs...."

GEORGES SIMENON
The Patience of Maigret

LAMB SHANKS WITH WHITE BEANS

✴✴ Lamb shanks have a deep lamb taste that I love, but after baking they look like something a Stone-Age hunter might gnaw on around the fire. To eliminate the primitive caveman look, cut the cooked meat off the bones in neat chunks and bury them in the bean mixture. As this bubbles merrily away in the oven, the kitchen will fill with the most tantalizing smells.

Serves 4–6

4 lamb shanks, well trimmed
Salt and freshly ground pepper to taste
2 tablespoons olive oil
4 large onions, coarsely chopped
2 stalks celery, coarsely chopped
2 large carrots, peeled and coarsely chopped
12 large garlic cloves, parboiled for 5 minutes
    and peeled
½ cup imported dry vermouth
1 cup stock
½ teaspoon dried thyme
1 teaspoon dried rosemary
2 cans cannellini beans, drained and rinsed
½ cup chopped parsley
½ tablespoon olive oil (optional)
2 large garlic cloves, crushed (optional)

1. Preheat the oven to 425°F. Line a baking sheet with aluminim foil, shiny side up. Place a rack on the baking sheet.

2. Place the lamb shanks on the rack and cook in the oven for 30 minutes, turning with tongs after 15 minutes. Blot on paper towels, and season with salt and pepper.

3. Meanwhile, heat the olive oil in a wide heavy skillet. Toss in the onions, celery, carrots, and garlic. Cover the skillet and steam over low heat for 10 minutes. Uncover, raise the heat, and sauté until the vegetables are beginning to brown.

4. Pour in the vermouth and bring to a boil, stirring and scraping the bottom of the pan with a wooden spoon. Add the stock, thyme, rosemary, and salt and pepper to taste. Scrape the mixture into a 9 x 13 x 2-inch baking pan. Place the shanks on the vegetables. Reduce the oven temperature to 350°F.

5. Cover the baking pan tightly with foil. Bake in the oven for ½ hour. Reduce oven temperature to 300°F. Bake for 1 hour more.

6. Remove the baking pan from the oven. Uncover, remove the shanks, and place them on a platter. Stir the beans and parsley into the pan liquid. Taste, and add more salt and pepper as needed. Return the shanks to the pot (turn them over, so that the side that was on top is now on the bottom), cover tightly, and bake for an additional ½ hour, until the shanks are very tender.

7. Cut the lamb off the bones in neat chunks. Bury the chunks in the bean mixture. The garlic will have imparted a magical sweetness to the bean mixture. If you want to add a stronger garlic taste, heat the additional ½ tablespoon olive oil and sauté the crushed garlic slowly until fragrant but not at all browned. Stir it into the stew. The stew may be served at once or stored in the refrigerator for a day or two.

LEFTOVERS

The best time to fully savor comfort food is the morning after. About 3:00 A.M., to be specific. Always cook enough comfort foods to ensure leftovers. Cover the leftovers well, or they will dry out and become discomforting. Position them in the refrigerator so that there is a certain sense of adventure in rooting them out during a post-midnight refrigerator forage, but not so that they are totally inaccessible. If you want the leftovers for a private guzzle, protect them from competing scavengers. Label the containers "Raw Chicken Livers" or "Tripe in Prune Sauce." Then, when you creep kitchenward in the silence of the sleeping house, your carefully hoarded cache of culinary treasure will be waiting just for you. All comfort foods are at their most delectably palatable at such moments, when the world is asleep, the sky outside is inky black, and the kitchen is in deep shadow. Leave the overhead light off. Open the refrigerator, and the light from the tiny bulb bathes you in a gentle glow. Don't even consider moving to the table and making busywork with plates, napkins, and flatware. Stand where you are and begin grazing. A generous pinch of meatball shedding gouts of solidified sauce; a solid wad of congealed pasta; a sliver of pot roast dripping gravy; a dollop of mousse scooped onto a finger; a cold, gob of bread pudding . . . ahhh!

VEAL BALLS IN RED PEPPER CREAM

✹✹ Meatballs are extremely comforting when things go wrong. These little veal balls are nestled in a creamy sauce with bits of sweet, fleshy red bell peppers. Homey and elegant at the same time, they will soothe your ruffled feelings. Share the dish with a few close friends, or save the leftovers to reheat at a later date. Better still, eat them right out of the refrigerator.

Makes 28 meatballs

2 pounds ground veal
2 eggs, lightly beaten
Salt and freshly ground pepper to taste
⅓ cup rice, parboiled in salted water for 10 minutes
¼ teaspoon grated nutmeg
2 tablespoons chopped fresh parsley
2 tablespoons chopped fresh dill
½ cup bread crumbs
5 teaspoons Hungarian paprika
2 tablespoons butter
6 large onions, coarsely chopped
12 red bell peppers, cut into coarse chunks
Chicken stock as needed
1 tablespoon flour
1 cup sour cream, at room temperature

1. Combine the veal, eggs, salt and pepper, rice, nutmeg, parsley, and dill. Use your hands to mix the ingredients well. Fry a tiny piece of the mixture in a skillet, taste it, and adjust the seasonings to your liking.

2. Preheat the oven to 400°F. Season the bread crumbs with salt, pepper, and 2 teaspoons of paprika. Form the meat mixture into 1½-inch-diameter balls. As they are formed, roll them in the flavored bread crumbs and place them on an ungreased baking sheet. You will have approximately 28 meatballs in all. Bake them in the oven for 20 minutes, turning them with tongs after the first 10 minutes.

3. Meanwhile melt the butter in a heavy stewpot. Toss in the onions. Cover and steam for 10 minutes. Uncover, raise the heat a bit, and stir in the pepper chunks. Cook until the onions are very tender and the peppers are beginning to get tender. Season with salt and pepper and stir in the remaining 1 tablespoon paprika. Stir over low heat until the vegetables are well coated with the paprika and it has lost its raw taste.

4. Reduce the oven temperature to 350°F. Put the browned veal balls on the onion mixture. Pour in stock to cover. Bake, covered, for 1 hour.

5. Stir the flour into the sour cream. Remove the casserole from the oven. Fish out the veal balls and put them on a platter. Stir a bit of the hot pan liquid into the sour cream. Stir the sour cream into the casserole. Taste and adjust seasoning. Return the veal balls to the casserole. Bring to a simmer, cover, and simmer for 5 to 10 minutes, until thickened and hot. The dish may be served at once or refrigerated for several days. Bring to room temperature before gently reheating.

POLENTA WITH ITALIAN SAUSAGE SAUCE OR MEATBALLS

✸✸ Polenta is cornmeal mush, a perfect bed for the kind of thick, spicy tomato sauce–based dishes that are out of fashion, yet so completely warm and comforting. Two examples are given here, a sauce containing Italian sausage and mushrooms and old-fashioned "Italian" meatballs. It pays to make each component of this recipe in bulk. The sausage sauce and the meatballs freeze well, and leftover polenta is delicious cut into strips and browned in butter. Cornmeal is currently enjoying a vogue. Comfort yourself and your friends with this heartwarming food.

Sausage Sauce
Makes approximately 10 cups

3 pounds Italian sausage with fennel seeds
    (half hot, half sweet)
4 large onions, coarsely chopped
4 garlic cloves, minced
2 large cans (1 pound 12 ounces each) Italian
    plum tomatoes, drained and crushed
    with your hands
1 can (6 ounces) tomato paste
½ cup imported dry vermouth
1 teaspoon dried basil
1 teaspoon dried oregano
½ cup fresh chopped parsley
Pinch of sugar
Salt and freshly ground pepper to taste
½ cup freshly grated Parmesan cheese
8 tablespoons (1 stick) butter
1 pound small mushrooms, quartered

51

1. Remove the sausage from its casing. Sauté the meat with the onions and garlic in a deep heavy pot. As the meat cooks, break it up with a wooden spoon. Dump the mixture into a colander to drain off all the fat, then return it to the pot.

2. Add the tomatoes, tomato paste, vermouth, herbs, sugar, salt and pepper, and Parmesan cheese. Simmer, partially covered, for ½ hour, until very thick.

3. Meanwhile, melt the butter in a skillet. Toss in the mushrooms. Cook until the mushrooms are tender. Scrape the mushrooms and their juices into the thick sausage sauce. Taste and adjust seasonings. The sauce may be stored in the refrigerator for several days, or in the freezer for several months. For maximum flavor, prepare it at least a day ahead of time.

Meatballs
Makes 35 meatballs

½ pound ground chuck
½ pound ground veal
½ pound ground pork
½ cup bread crumbs
½ cup grated Parmesan cheese
2 eggs, lightly beaten
½ teaspoon crushed fennel seeds
½ cup chopped fresh parsley
¼ cup chopped fresh basil
Salt and freshly ground pepper to taste
2 tablespoons olive oil
2 onions, coarsely chopped
3 garlic cloves, crushed

2 cans (1 pound 12 ounces each) Italian plum
    tomatoes, drained and crushed with
    your hands
1 can (6 ounces) tomato paste
½ cup dry red wine
¼ cup grated Parmesan cheese
¼ teaspoon fennel seeds
½ teaspoon dried basil
½ teaspoon dried oregano
½ cup chopped parsley

1. Combine the meats, crumbs, and cheese. Add the eggs, crushed fennel, fresh parsley, and basil, and salt and pepper. Use your hands to mix it thoroughly. In a small skillet, fry a tiny piece of the mixture and taste it. Adjust the seasoning to your liking. Shape into 35 balls about 1 inch in diameter.

2. In a heavy skillet, brown the meatballs in their own fat on all sides. When they are browned, blot them on paper towels and pour the fat from the skillet.

3. In the same skillet, heat the olive oil. Toss in the onions and sauté, scraping the bottom of the skillet with a wooden spoon. When they are almost tender, stir in the garlic and sauté for a few more minutes. Stir in the remaining ingredients and salt and pepper to taste.

4. Combine the meatballs and sauce in a casserole. Simmer, covered, for 20 to 25 minutes, until the meatballs are cooked through and the sauce is very thick.

Polenta

Serves 12

1 ½ cups yellow cornmeal
8 cups chicken stock
12 tablespoons (1 ½ sticks) butter, cut into
    pieces
½ cup grated Parmesan cheese
Salt and freshly ground pepper to taste

1. Combine the cornmeal and 2 cups stock, stirring well with a whisk to prevent lumps.

2. In a heavy saucepan, bring the remaining 6 cups stock to a boil. Pour in the cornmeal mixture, whisking constantly. Reduce the heat to low, and cook, stirring with a wooden spoon, for about 15 minutes, until the polenta is thick and tender. Remove from the heat.

3. Stir in the butter, Parmesan cheese, and pepper. Taste, and add salt if necessary.

4. Serve at once by ladling a generous amount of hot polenta onto each plate. Top with a serving of meatballs or sausage sauce. Pass additional Parmesan cheese at the table.

MEAT LOAF

✹✹✹ Don't assume that meat loaf is lowly food, and that guests at your table will burst into derisive laughter the moment you place one in front of them. I find that people, no matter how "gourmet," harbor a deep hankering for this homey dish. "Oh, I *love* meat loaf," they gasp, starry-eyed, as the beautiful plump loaf is borne to the table. Plan on plenty of leftovers. Cold, thin slices of this loaf are delicious on slices of fresh, crusty rye bread.

Serves 8–10

1 pound sweet Italian sausage with fennel
    seeds
1 pound ground veal
1 pound ground beef chuck
2 cups bread crumbs
2 eggs, lightly beaten
Salt and freshly ground pepper to taste
2 large garlic cloves, crushed
¼ cup dry red wine
½ cup chopped fresh parsley
1 can (1 pound 12 ounces) Italian plum to-
    matoes
1 lemon

1. Preheat the oven to 350°F.

2. Combine the meats, bread crumbs, eggs, salt and pepper, garlic, wine, and parsley. Drain the tomatoes, reserving the juice. Crush the tomatoes with your hands and add to the meats. Add approximately two thirds of the tomato juice. Use a lemon zester to

grate the rind of the lemon over the meat mixture (so that both the rind and the lemon oil go in). Use your hands to combine the ingredients very well. Fry a small piece of the mixture in a small skillet, taste for seasoning, and adjust to your liking.

3. Lightly oil a shallow square baking dish. Form the meat into a compact plump loaf, about 9 x 6½ inches. Place it in the baking dish. Bake for 1½ to 1¾ hours, until an instant-read thermometer inserted in the loaf registers 170°F. There is no need to baste the loaf during the baking time, but do drain or spoon off the fat two or three times.

4. Let the baking pan cool on a rack for ½ hour before slicing the meat loaf.

"If meatloaves do not qualify as food for the gods, then pity the poor gods."

CRAIG CLAIBORNE
Kitchen Primer

OLD-FASHIONED POT ROAST

★★★ "This tastes like home!" blurted a guest at my table when she tasted my pot roast. I swear, there were tears in her eyes. This reminds everyone of happy childhood days on the farm, even if they grew up in the middle of the city.

Serves 6–8

1 first-cut brisket (about 4 pounds), trimmed of all but a thin layer of top fat
1 tablespoon butter
1 onion, halved and sliced into thin half-moons
¼ cup brandy
¼ cup tomato paste
Salt and freshly ground pepper to taste
½ cup beef or chicken stock
4 large garlic cloves, peeled and left whole
1 carrot, peeled and sliced
1 stalk celery with leaves, sliced
3 sprigs parsley
8 whole carrots, peeled and trimmed

1. Preheat the oven to 350°F.

2. In a large skillet, sear the brisket in its own fat, beginning fat side down. When the meat is browned on both sides, put it on a platter and loosely cover it with foil.

3. Pour beef drippings out of the skillet but do not wipe out the skillet. Melt the butter in the skillet. Sauté the onion. When it is almost tender, pour in the brandy. Boil, scraping the pan with a wooden spoon to release all the browned bits. When the brandy has cooked away, stir in the tomato paste. Season with a bit of salt and freshly ground pepper. Scrape

the mixture into a 9 x 13 x 2-inch baking pan. Pour the stock over the onion.

4. Season the meat on both sides with salt and pepper. Place the meat, fat side up, on the onion. Pour in any meat juices that have accumulated on the platter. Tuck the garlic, carrot and celery slices, and parsley around the meat. Cover the baking pan tightly with heavy-duty aluminim foil.

5. Place the baking dish in the oven for 1 hour. Reduce the oven temperature to 250°F and bake for an additional hour.

6. Uncover the baking pan, arrange the whole carrots around the brisket, salt and pepper them lightly, and re-cover. Return to the oven for another ½ hour, or until the meat and carrots are tender.

7. To serve, slice the meat against the grain and serve with the carrots and gravy. If desired, the gravy may be puréed in a food processor or pushed through a fine sieve. If you choose to serve the gravy unpuréed, discard the parsley and celery leaves. The meat slices may be refrigerated in the gravy and reheated in a day or so.

HONEY-MUSTARD CHICKEN

✱The ravishing, well-loved combination of honey and mustard gives these chicken breasts their golden, sweet-hot glaze. Do not overcook the chicken, or it will lose the bursting juiciness that makes it so special.

Serves 6

6 chicken breast halves (about ½ pound each)
Salt and freshly ground pepper
Juice of 1 large lemon
2 tablespoons oil
Several dashes Tabasco sauce
3 garlic cloves, peeled and crushed
½ teaspoon powdered ginger
½ cup clover honey

½ cup Dijon mustard
½ tablespoon soy sauce

1. Preheat the oven to 350°F.

2. Line a baking sheet with aluminum foil, shiny side up. Place a wire rack on the sheet. Arrange the chicken breasts, skin side up, on the rack. Season with salt and pepper.

3. Beat together the remaining ingredients. Taste, and add salt and pepper if necessary. Brush the chicken breasts with half of the honey-mustard sauce. Put in the oven and bake for 20 minutes.

4. Remove from the oven. Brush with the remaining sauce. Return to the oven and bake for an additional 20 minutes, or until just done. Serve at once.

CHICKEN POT PIE

✿✿ More shades of happy childhood. A chicken pot pie is basic "mother food." Frozen puff pastry makes a very easy, stress-free flaky topping.

Serves 6

2 chickens, 3 pounds each
2 onions, sliced
2 carrots, sliced
2 cups chopped celery and celery leaves
Salt and freshly ground pepper to taste
2 cups fresh or thawed frozen peas
½ pound mushrooms, sliced
1 cup heavy cream
6 tablespoons butter, softened
6 tablespoons flour
½ package frozen puff pastry (1 sheet)
1 egg, beaten

1. Put the chickens in a large pot with the onions, carrots, celery, and just enough water to cover. Bring to a boil, skim off foam and scum, and reduce the heat to a simmer. Add pepper and a bit of salt, cover, and cook for 45 to 60 minutes, until the chickens are tender and succulent. Let cool in the stock.

2. Remove the chickens from the stock. Strain the stock, pour it into a jar, and leave in the freezer while you bone and skin the chickens. Tear the chicken meat into large chunks. Mix the meat with the celery and carrots from the stock, the peas, and the mushrooms.

3. Remove the stock from the freezer and skim off most of the fat. Use a little of the stock to moisten the chicken. Cover the chicken.

4. In a saucepan, boil the stock until reduced to about 3 cups. Stir in the cream. Blend the butter and flour to make a paste and add it to the simmering stock. Stir until thickened, then stir in the chicken and vegetables. Taste and adjust seasonings. Pour the mixture into a 2-quart casserole dish.

5. Preheat the oven to 400°F.

6. Thaw the frozen sheet of pastry according to package directions, and unfold it. Moisten the edges of the casserole. Lay the sheet of pastry over the casserole and trim to fit. Press the edges lightly to seal. Brush with beaten egg.

7. Reroll any pastry scraps and cut them into the shape of a chicken or into leaf shapes. Place the decorations on top of the main crust and brush with egg. Make a hole in the center for steam to escape.

8. Bake for 30 to 40 minutes, until rich, puffed, and brown.

CANTONESE STEAMED CHICKEN WITH MUSHROOMS AND SAUSAGE

✤When I've had a high-stress day and feel the need for some pampering, I often head to First China Restaurant in Doraville, Georgia, for a dish of this chicken and a glass of Chinese beer. Eddie Mui, the chef member of the family that runs the restaurant, was kind enough to contribute the recipe for this collection. You will need a wok with a steamer rack and a cover.

Serves 2–3

16 ounces boneless, skinless chicken breast
5 dried Chinese mushrooms, soaked, drained, and cut into 1-inch pieces
1 Chinese sausage, thinly sliced on the diagonal
4 scallions, cut into 2-inch pieces
1 2½-inch-thick piece of ginger, peeled and very thinly sliced
1½ tablespoons cornstarch
Salt to taste
½ tablespoon sugar
½ tablespoon soy sauce
1 tablespoon oyster sauce
½ teaspoon light sesame oil
Ground white pepper to taste
1 tablespoon dry sherry
1 tablespoon peanut oil

1. Remove every bit of fat and gristle from the chicken. Slant-cut the chicken into 1-inch pieces. Set aside. Combine the mushrooms, sausage, scallions, and ginger. Set aside.

2. Combine the cornstarch and ½ tablespoon cold water, stirring well to dissolve the cornstarch. Stir in the remaining ingredients except the peanut oil.

3. Toss the chicken with the liquid mixture. Toss in the peanut oil. Toss in the mushroom-sausage mixture and 3 tablespoons cold water.

4. Spread the mixture in an even layer on a china plate that fits in the wok. Put some water in the wok and put the steamer rack in place. Bring to a boil. Place the plate on the rack, cover the wok, and steam over boiling water for 12 minutes, or until the chicken is opaque and *just* done. Serve at once, with white rice.

BRAISED VEAL SHANK

✹✹ Osso buco is the best-known veal shank recipe, but there are countless other ways of preparing this succulent cut of meat. Veal shanks make an outstanding veal stew, and diners have the lagniappe of the delicious cache of marrow hidden in the bone.

Serves 6

Flour
Salt and freshly ground pepper to taste
3 tablespoons vegetable oil
1 hind veal shank, sliced about 1½ inches
    thick (6–7 slices)
2 tablespoons butter
2 large onions, halved and sliced into thick
    half-moons
1 cup dry white wine
3 garlic cloves, crushed
1 3-inch piece of orange rind
2 tablespoons brandy
Veal or chicken stock, as needed
½ teaspoon dried thyme
1 teaspoon dried tarragon

1. Spread the flour on a sheet of wax paper. Season it with salt and pepper.

2. Heat the oil in a wide, deep, nonreactive skillet. Dredge the shanks in the seasoned flour, shaking off the excess. Sauté them over medium heat until well browned on both sides. Transfer to a platter.

3. Pour all fat from the skillet. Add the butter and let melt. Stir in the onions. Let them cook gently until tender.

4. Pour in the wine and bring to a boil. Let boil for 2 to 3 minutes, stirring and scraping the bottom of the skillet.

5. Return the shanks to the skillet. Add the garlic, orange rind, brandy, and enough stock to barely cover the meat. Crumble the herbs between your fingers and add them to the skillet. Bring to a simmer. Cover and simmer gently for 30 minutes.

6. Uncover and turn the shanks over. Cover and simmer gently for 40 minutes to 1 hour, until the shanks are meltingly tender and beginning to separate from the bones, and the liquid has cooked down to a thick rich sauce. Taste and adjust seasonings. Serve with buttered rice and small spoons or forks for digging the marrow out of the bones. If necessary, this dish can be prepared a few hours ahead of time. Let sit, partially covered. At serving time reheat very gently.

"Who can fail to recall the experience of entering a home or small restaurant where an honest, soul warming stew has been simmering for hours?"

JAMES VILLAS
American Taste

58

Pasta, Grains, and Breads

**"Everybody has some special food
that makes them feel taken care of,
a culinary escape from danger."**

JANE and MICHAEL STERN
Square Meals

MACARONI AND CHEESE

✭✭✭ How pleasant to chase the mubblefubbles by downing spoonfuls of this ineffably soothing stuff. It is nursery food at its most magnificent. I used to make very fancy versions of macaroni and cheese until I read Pearl Bailey's remarkable book, *Pearl's Kitchen*. She waxes poetic (with good reason) about her M & C, but gives almost no measurements. Here it is, all worked out—basic, no-frills macaroni and cheese that I can't recommend highly enough.

Serves a small army

2 pounds elbow macaroni
1 cup melted butter (2 sticks)
Salt and freshly ground pepper to taste
1½–2 pounds sharp cheddar cheese, cut into
    chunks
Approximately 7 cups milk

1. Preheat the oven to 350°F.

2. Boil the macaroni until about two-thirds done. Pour into a colander. Rinse well under cold running water, stirring the pasta around with your hands so that the water reaches all of it.

3. Put the macaroni in a large roasting pan.

(I use an old-fashioned speckled roaster.) Toss with the melted butter. Season with a bit of salt and plenty of pepper. With your hands, thoroughly mix in the cheese. Pour in milk to just barely cover the macaroni.

4. Cook, uncovered, for ½ hour, or until the cheese begins to melt. Pull out the pan and stir everything up very well with a wooden spoon, so that the melting cheese is evenly distributed through the macaroni. Taste and adjust the seasoning, adding as much salt and pepper as necessary. Return the pan to the oven and cook, uncovered, for approximately 1 hour, until it is browned on top and the milk has been absorbed. Serve at once.

5. Store leftovers, in the covered roasting pan, in the refrigerator. To reheat, slice a hunk off the congealed mass. Put it in a skillet with a little milk or half-and-half. Cover and heat slowly, turning once with a broad spatula. Macaroni and cheese is even better reheated than on the first day, and it's absolutely divine cold, right out of the refrigerated pan.

> **"I have always maintained that there is nothing wrong with nursery food now that we are grown up and can have a glass of wine with it."**
> ELIZABETH RAY
> **in *Writers' Favorite Recipes***

LEMON-BUTTER ANGEL HAIR

✸✸✸ When you need solace in a hurry, when you want to whip up something to cry into, make this fast, unutterably comforting pasta pilaf from my friend and colleague, Christianne Lauterbach. If you wish to comfort your family and friends as well, the recipe can be multiplied.

Serves 1

2 tablespoons butter
2 ounces angel hair pasta
1 cup hot chicken stock
Freshly ground pepper to taste
Lemon juice to taste

1. Melt the butter in a small pot. Break up the pasta. Toss the pasta in the butter until it is well coated.

2. Pour in the hot stock and grind in the pepper. Cover and cook over very low heat for 10 minutes, or until all the liquid is absorbed.

3. Squeeze in the lemon juice (I use the juice of 1 small lemon) and serve at once.

PANTRY THERAPY

There are times when made-from-scratch comfort foods won't do at all. When you're all alone and the blues strike, the pantry shelf is always there with its neat rows of cans and packages, sending out seductive messages of comfort and joy.

A steam-wreathed mug full of milky Campbell's tomato soup brimming over with crumbled saltines; a nice cup of hot cocoa in which a fat marshmallow bobs, slowly melting into luscious swirls; a welcoming bowl of "Kraft Dinner"—tender elbow macaroni nestled in the creamy embrace of that inimitable Kraft processed cheese-milk-butter sauce; fingers of buttered, cinnamon-sprinkled toast, slowly sogging into a shallow bowl of gently warmed chocolate milk. It's okay. Don't feel guilty. Everyone indulges in pantry therapy at one time or another. It is a particularly potent evocation of childhood and perfect for the lonesome megrims. Just don't boast about it to your best gourmet friends.

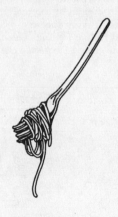

SAVORY RICE PUDDING

✖✖ Rice pudding does not have to be sweet. This savory version is a creamy mass of tender grains and melted cheese. It's excellent with meat loaf or pot roast, or all by itself for a profoundly tranquilizing culinary respite from the world.

Serves 6

3 tablespoons butter
6 scallions, thinly sliced
1 garlic clove, crushed
1 cup long-grain rice
2 ½ cups boiling chicken stock
½ cup imported dry white vermouth
Salt and freshly ground pepper to taste
1 ½ cups sour cream, at room temperature
¾ cup diced Gruyère cheese
¾ cup diced Italian fontina cheese
3 tablespoons grated Parmesan cheese

1. Preheat the oven to 350°F.

2. Heat the butter in a 1 ½-quart pot. Sauté the scallions and garlic until limp but not at all browned.

3. Stir in the rice. Toss until coated with butter. Stir in the boiling stock, the wine, and a bit of salt and pepper. Immediately cover the pot and place it in the oven for 15 to 20 minutes, until the liquid is almost all absorbed.

4. Butter a 2-quart casserole. Toss the rice with the sour cream and the cheeses. Increase the oven temperature to 400°F.

5. Spoon the rice into the buttered dish. Bake, uncovered, for ½ hour. Serve at once.

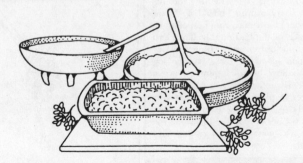

CUSTARDY CORN BREAD

✳✳ This is wonderful with chili, or for breakfast with bacon on the side. It's really a cross between a spoon bread and a Tex-Mex corn bread.

Serves 6

1 can (16 ounces) creamed corn
1 cup cornmeal
3 eggs, lightly beaten
1 teaspoon salt
½ teaspoon baking soda
¾ cup buttermilk
5 tablespoons melted butter
1 can (4 ounces) chopped green chilies, well
    drained
2 cups grated sharp cheddar cheese
2 tablespoons butter

1. Preheat the oven to 400°F.

2. Combine the corn, cornmeal, eggs, salt, baking soda, buttermilk, and melted butter in a large bowl. Stir in the chilies and 1 cup cheese.

3. Put the 2 tablespoons butter in a 1½–2 quart round ovenproof casserole. Put it in the oven until the butter is melted and hot. Immediately pour in the batter. Sprinkle with the remaining cheese.

4. Bake for 35 to 40 minutes, until golden brown and set. Serve warm, right out of the casserole.

RAISIN BREAD

✱✱ The whole process of bread baking is therapeutic, from the kneading through the rising of the dough to the odorous baking. Of course, the eating is best of all. You may have to hire an armed guard to fend off the hungry hordes while the bread cools.

Makes 2 loaves

2 packages yeast
1 cup warm milk (110°-115°F)
1 teaspoon salt
½ cup sugar
1 teaspoon vanilla extract
4–5 cups unbleached white flour
3 eggs
8 tablespoons (1 stick) butter, softened and
　　cut into pieces
½ cup raisins, soaked in warm water to cover
4 tablespoons melted butter

1. Combine the yeast and warm milk. Mix with a whisk or a small fork to dissolve the yeast.

2. Stir in the salt, sugar, vanilla, 2 cups flour, and eggs.

3. Beat in the remaining flour, 1 cup at a time, to make a medium-soft dough. In the bowl, knead in the butter.

4. Knead the dough in the bowl for 10 min-utes, until satiny, elastic, but somewhat sticky.

5. Remove the dough from the bowl, cover with a towel, and let it rest while you wash, dry, and butter the bowl. Put the dough in the bowl, turn to coat with butter, cover with plastic wrap, and set in a warm, draft-free place to double in bulk. This will take about 2 hours.

6. When doubled, flour your fist and punch down the dough. Drain the raisins, spread out on a paper towel, and pat dry. Knead the raisins thoroughly into the dough.

7. Grease two 9 x 5 x 3-inch loaf pans.

8. Divide the dough into two parts. Keep one covered. Roll out the dough into an oval about ¼ inch thick. Starting with the narrow end of the oval, roll it like a jelly roll. Place the roll, seam side down, in one of the loaf pans. Repeat with the second piece of dough. Cover both with plastic wrap and put in a warm, draft-free place to double in bulk, about 30 to 45 minutes.

9. Preheat oven to 350°F.

10. When doubled, gently brush the tops with melted butter. Put the pans in the oven. Bake for 35 to 40 minutes, or until the bread is browned and a knuckle thump on the bot-tom produces a hollow sound. Brush the tops with melted butter once again. Remove from the pans and let cool on a rack.

Vegetables

"...A good meal in troubled times
is always that much salvage from
disaster."

A. J. Liebling

SCALLIONS ON RED PEPPER PURÉE

✱✱ The colors, the very gentle on-iony flavor, and the texture contrast of the scallions against the purée make this a particularly potent comfort food. Serve it as a separate course and forget the forks. Pick up each scallion, dab it in the purée, and eat happily.

Serves 6

Red Pepper Purée

Makes approximately 2 cups

2 tablespoons butter
6 red bell peppers, chopped
1½ cups chicken stock
Salt and freshly ground black pepper to taste
¼ cup heavy cream

1. Melt the butter. Toss the bell peppers in the butter. Stir in the stock. Simmer for 20 minutes, until the peppers are tender. Season with salt and black pepper.

2. Purée the pepper mixture in a blender or food processor. Push the puréed mixture through a sieve to rid it of pepper skins. Pour the mixture into a saucepan, stir in the cream, and simmer gently until it is thick enough to coat a spoon. Taste and adjust the seasonings. Keep the sauce warm while you prepare the scallions. (The sauce may be made in advance and refrigerated.)

Scallions

Approximately 36 thin scallions, trimmed of their "beards" and all but 2 inches of the green
8 tablespoons (1 stick) butter

1. Wash the scallions. Shake them dry. Some water will still cling to each scallion.

2. Melt the butter in a heavy skillet. When the butter is hot, toss in the scallions so that they are well coated with butter. Arrange the scallions so that they all face in one direction. Clap the cover on the skillet, turn off the light, and let sit for 3 to 5 minutes, until the scallions are tender but not mushy.

TO SERVE If possible, choose clear glass or white china plates. Pour a neat puddle of pepper purée in the center of each plate. With tongs, remove the scallions from their butter and neatly place several scallions in the center of each puddle. Serve at once. (The scallion butter, which is now delicately onion-flavored, can be refrigerated and saved for a later use.) As a change, try steamed asparagus spears served in the same way.

TOMATO PUDDING

✱✱ This is a very old recipe, almost forgotten today. The flavor is vividly sweet and sour. Sometimes I put a dab of sour cream on each serving. Should you have any left over, the pudding makes a spectacular cold dish, too.

Serves 4–6

8 slices whole-wheat bread, toasted and cubed (about 4 cups)
8 tablespoons (1 stick) butter
¾ cup thinly sliced scallions
2½ cups tomato purée
1 cup brown sugar
Salt to taste
Fresh lemon juice
Sour cream (optional)

1. Preheat the oven to 375°F.

2. Butter a 1½-quart 8-inch square baking dish. Spread the bread cubes in the dish.

3. Melt the butter in a saucepan. Toss in the scallions and stir until heated through but not limp.

4. Add the tomato purée, sugar, and salt. Stir in lemon juice to taste. The amount needed to provide a good balance of sweet and sour will depend on the acidity of the tomato purée. Bring to a boil, stirring. Pour the mixture over the bread. Stir to combine.

5. Bake for 35 minutes. Serve hot. Pass the sour cream.

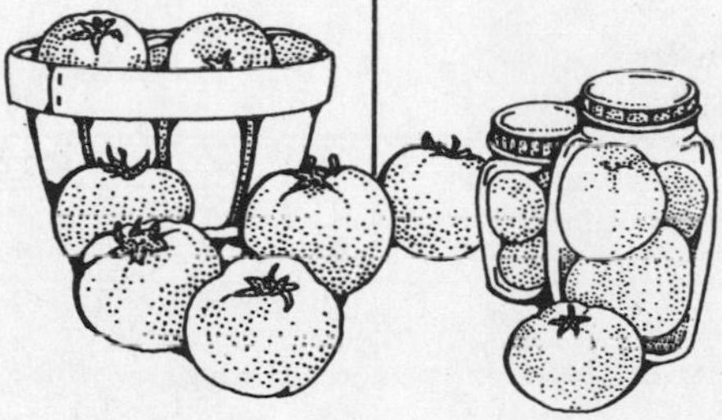

CORN PUDDING

✖✖ Don't make this Southern-style pudding with fresh corn unless the ears were picked just before cooking. Without the sugar, the pudding is no longer typical of the American South, and it will not be quite so creamy and tender, but sugarphobes can leave it out and still have a decent (but not perfect) dish. Plan on leftovers; corn pudding is as seductive cold as it is hot. In fact, it's a lovely picnic dish.

Serves 8

4 cups frozen corn kernels, thawed
4 tablespoons butter
½ cup sliced scallions
8 eggs
1½ cups half-and-half
3 tablespoons sugar (optional)
Salt and freshly ground pepper to taste
Several dashes Tabasco sauce

1. Preheat the oven to 325°F.

2. In a food processor fitted with the steel blade, chop half of the corn. Combine the chopped and unchopped corn. Spread the corn in a well-buttered 9 x 13 x 2-inch baking dish.

3. Melt the butter. Sauté the scallions until limp but not browned. Add them to the corn.

4. Beat the eggs lightly. Beat in the half-and-half, sugar, salt and pepper, and Tabasco. Pour the mixture over the corn and scallions.

5. Bake for 30 to 35 minutes, or until just barely set. Let the pudding sit on a rack for 10 minutes before serving.

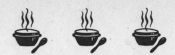

FRIED GREEN TOMATOES

*** Fried tomatoes are extraordinary. The combination of crusty, firm tomatoes and creamy pan gravy has to be tasted to be believed. It's impossible to feel sorry for yourself while eating food like this. Sometimes a few hard, thoroughly green tomatoes show up in the produce department of the supermarket. Of course, if you grow your own you can have this small feast frequently.

Serves 2–4

½ cup flour
Salt and freshly ground pepper to taste
4 green tomatoes
4 tablespoons butter
1 tablespoon oil
2 tablespoons brown sugar
¾ cup heavy cream

1. Season the flour with salt and pepper and spread it on a sheet of wax paper.

2. Slice the tomatoes ¼ inch thick. Dredge each slice in the seasoned flour and place on a rack.

3. Heat the butter and oil in a large, heavy skillet. When very hot, sauté the tomatoes until crusty on one side. Turn the slices, sprinkle with a bit of brown sugar, and sauté until crusty on the second side. Blot the bottom side on a double thickness of paper towels and place the tomatoes on a platter. Repeat until all the slices are sautéed. Add a little oil and butter as needed, but not too much; the pan should be just about dry by the time the tomatoes are done.

4. Pour the cream into the skillet. Bring to a boil and boil for a few minutes, stirring and scraping the bottom of the skillet with a wooden spoon, until the cream forms a thick sauce. Season with salt and pepper. Pour the sauce over the tomatoes (use a rubber spatula to scrape out every delicious bit) and serve at once.

POTATO-ONION-GARLIC GRATIN

✹✹✹ Don't be frightened. Long baking renders both the garlic and the onion sweet and mild. The finished dish will be the most compelling, mysterious, and hard-to-stop-eating mashed potato casserole you have ever tasted.

Serves 4–6

2 large heads garlic
2 large sweet onions
4 large Idaho potatoes
Salt and freshly ground pepper to taste
1 cup grated Gruyère cheese
1 cup heavy cream

1. Preheat the oven to 425°F.

2. Remove the outer papery covering of the garlic heads, but do not peel and do not separate the cloves. Wrap the garlic heads well in heavy-duty foil. Put them in the oven. Put the onions on a doubled sheet of heavy-duty foil, but do not wrap them. Put them in the oven. Pierce the potatoes in several places with a thin skewer or the tines of a fork. Put them directly on the oven rack. Bake the garlic for 1 hour and the onions and potatoes for 1¼ hours.

3. After 1 hour, pull out the package of garlic heads, unwrap, and let cool for 5 minutes. Separate the cloves and squeeze them over a bowl so that the softened garlic pops into the bowl.

4. After 1¼ hours, pull out the onions and potatoes. If the onions are not very soft, almost collapsed, put them back in for a few minutes. Perforate the potatoes lengthwise and breadthwise with the tines of a fork and squeeze. Scoop the potato flesh into a bowl and mash it with a potato masher. (Save the skins for a special nibble. See note.)

5. With a sharp knife, cut off the stem and root end of the onions. Remove the skin and first layer. Put the onions in the container of a food processor and purée.

6. Combine the mashed potato, softened garlic, puréed onions, and salt and pepper in the bowl of an electric mixer, preferably fitted with a paddle attachment. Beat them together until smooth and blended. Scrape the mixture into a gratin dish. Sprinkle the top with grated Gruyère cheese. (The recipe may be prepared in advance to this point and refrigerated, covered, for a day or so. Bring to room temperature before proceeding.)

7. Reduce the oven temperature to 350°F. Pour the cream over the mixture. Bake, un-

70

covered, for 40 to 50 minutes, until the top is browned and bubbly and the cream has cooked down to a very thick saucelike consistency. Try to arrange to have some leftovers; this is very exciting when it's cold.

NOTE The skins may be refrigerated, well wrapped, until needed. When you are ready for your nibble, cut them into strips. Place them, skin side down, on a baking sheet. Drizzle with melted butter and sprinkle with Parmesan cheese. Bake in a 400°F oven until crisp.

> **"The discovery of a new dish does more for the happiness of mankind than the discovery of a new star."**
> JEAN ANTHELME BRILLAT-SAVARIN
> *The Physiology of Taste*

BABY LIMAS IN CREAM

✶✶ If you wish, serve these creamy beans as an accompaniment to a roast or some lamb chops, but they are really at their best all alone. With Mozart on the phonograph, a good book propped up in front of you, and a bowl of these beans at hand, the universe is a friendly place.

Serves 4–6

1 bag (1 pound) frozen baby lima beans
1 cup chicken stock
¼ teaspoon dried thyme
Freshly ground pepper to taste
½ cup heavy cream
Salt to taste

1. Put the partially thawed limas in a heavy deep skillet. Pour in the stock and season with thyme and pepper. Cover, bring to a boil, and boil for 5 minutes.

2. Stir in the cream. Return to a boil, covered. Uncover and boil until the liquid has cooked down to almost nothing and the beans are tender. If the liquid cooks down before the beans are done, add more stock.

3. Taste and add salt if necessary. Serve piping-hot.

ARTICHOKE GRATIN

✦Some vegetables are horrid when frozen (asparagus, broccoli); others are amazingly good (kernel corn, artichoke hearts). Imagine the time it would take to make this gratin with fresh artichokes! There is terrific texture in this dish, because the cheese and crumbs form patches of crisp crust.

Serves 8

4 packages frozen artichoke hearts, thawed
1 cup bread crumbs
1 cup grated Parmesan cheese
½ cup melted butter (1 stick)
2 tablespoons chopped fresh parsley
Salt and freshly ground pepper to taste
½ lemon
Lemon wedges

1. Preheat the oven to 350°F.

2. Combine all the ingredients except lemon in a bowl. With a citrus zester, grate the rind of the lemon right over the bowl (so that the rind and some of the lemon oil go in). Toss everything together very well.

3. Pour and scrape the mixture into a 9 x 13 x 2-inch baking dish. Bake for 45 minutes, until browned and crusty. Squeeze the juice of the half lemon over the gratin and serve at once with lemon wedges.

CHÈVRE

If the thought of goat cheese conjures up visions of smelly stables and smellier cheeses, think again. Fresh chèvres (French-type goat's milk cheeses) are the most seductively creamy, delicate, and soothing of cheeses. Their goaty origin is evident in a delicious and subtle tanginess. If you are comforting yourself with chèvre for the first time, eat it plain. Let the cheese sit for an hour or so, until it is at room temperature; then spread some on a piece of crusty French bread, a slice of toasted rye, or a bagel. The first taste is a revelation, the second a compulsion; it is all too easy to devour a whole log in one sitting, and then to look around, wishing for more. As good as chèvre plain is chèvre hot and melting into other ingredients in a cooked dish. For a graphic and simple example, toss some crumbled Boucheron or Montrachet into a bowl of just cooked and drained *al dente* pasta shells along with some melted butter and a touch of heavy cream. The pasta must be hot so that the cheese, butter, and cream melt together to surround and fill the pasta with a glorious creaminess. Or heat a can of black bean soup until piping-hot and pour into a pottery bowl. Crumble some Boucheron or Montrachet and scatter it over the surface of the soup. Stir gently, so that the soup is marbled with swirls of melting chèvre. Both of these simple dishes are the sort of thing you eat with a soup spoon, sighing blissfully between mouthfuls. What makes them even more comforting is that chèvre, for all its mouth-filling richness, is low-fat and low-calorie.

GREEN BEAN SALAD WITH CHÈVRE

To me, this salad is supremely comforting, because I love chèvre and I love the gentle acidity of sherry vinegar. The crisp green beans bathed in vinegar and tossed with goat cheese makes a combination I find irresistible and totally soothing. If chèvre is not available, feta cheese can be substituted, although the stress-reducing level of the recipe will then be lessened.

Serves 4

1 pound blanched, cooled green beans
1 small onion, minced
½ cup grated Parmesan cheese
6 tablespoons olive oil
2 tablespoons sherry vinegar
Salt and freshly ground pepper to taste
6 ounces chèvre, crumbled
Watercress
Greek olives
Halved cherry tomatoes

1. Toss the green beans with onion and Parmesan cheese.

2. In a small bowl, combine the olive oil, sherry vinegar, and salt and pepper. Pour this dressing over the bean mixture.

3. Add the crumbled chèvre and toss together carefully. Try to avoid breaking up the pieces of cheese.

4. Arrange on watercress. Garnish with black olives and tomatoes.

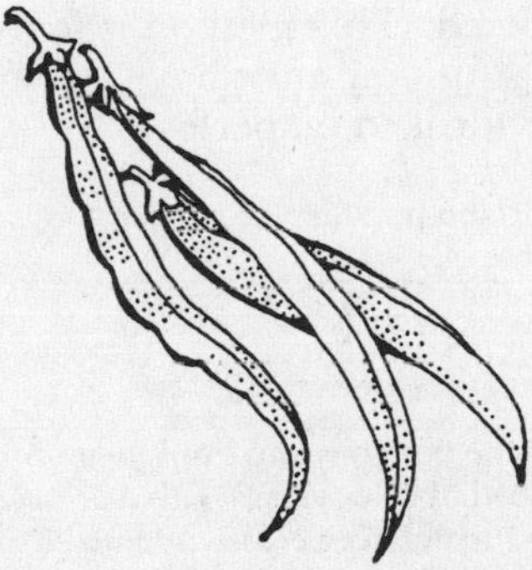

OLD-FASHIONED FRIED POTATOES

✴✴✴ Does anyone remember old-fashioned fried potatoes? They pre-date the matchstick-thin fries so popular today in fast-food franchises. Crinkle-cut, golden and crunchy-crisp on the outside, fluffy-white and floury within, they were almost addictive in their goodness. I have devised an excellent and easy home method of turning out these almost forgotten fries that doesn't involve deep frying at all. The potatoes, after peeling and cutting, are oven fried. This method is fool-proof, but you must have a crinkle cutter for it to be perfect.

Large Idaho potatoes
Vegetable oil
Salt

1. Preheat the oven to 450°F.

2. Peel the potatoes and drop them into a large bowl of cold water. With a crinkle cutter, cut the potatoes crosswise into ½-inch-thick slices. Cut each slice in half vertically. As they are cut, return them to the bowl of cold water.

3. You will need a metal roasting or baking pan, about 2½ inches deep, of a size to hold the potatoes in one layer without crowding. (If they are crowded they will steam rather than fry.) Pour in oil to a depth of ¼ inch. Heat in the oven until it *just* reaches the smoking point.

4. Meanwhile, drain and dry the potatoes very well. (If they are at all wet, they will splatter when they hit the oil.) *As soon* as the oil begins to smoke (you will smell it), spread the potatoes out in the pan. Let bake for 30 minutes.

5. Stir the potatoes around in the oil and spread out again. Let bake for an additional 20 to 30 minutes, shaking the pan and stirring occasionally, until they are golden brown and crisp on the outside.

6. Scoop out the potatoes with a skimmer or slotted spoon. Drain well on paper towels, sprinkle with salt, and serve at once.

NOTE This recipe can be prepared with sweet potatoes, with excellent results.

Desserts

**"... When I get unhappy
I don't merely tear my hair
I tear into 3 dozen Mallomars"**
JUDITH VIORST
*How Did I Get to Be 40
and Other Atrocities*

APPLE CRUMBLE

★★★ This old-fashioned, classic American dessert has enough texture, taste, and temperature contrasts to knock your socks off. It will assuage a battered psyche and make you feel well protected from the vagaries of a sometimes unfair fate. It is especially good for gastronomes who are fed up with nouvelle desserts that feature trembling, gossamer mousses on anemic puddles of pallid sauce. Apple crumble will reestablish faith in gutsy, down-to-earth food.

Serves 6

Juice and rind of 1 small lemon
8 Granny Smith apples
1¼ cups firmly packed dark brown sugar
½ teaspoon cinnamon
1 cup sifted flour
Pinch of salt
½ cup ground pecans
8 tablespoons (1 stick) butter, softened
1 pint vanilla ice cream
2–4 tablespoons Frangelico (optional)

1. Preheat the oven to 350°F.

2. Put the lemon juice and rind in a bowl.

3. Peel and core the apples and slice them into ¼-inch wedges. As they are sliced, toss the wedges into the lemon juice. Toss in ¼ cup sugar and the cinnamon.

4. Butter a shallow baking dish. Spread in the apple mixture.

5. Combine the remaining sugar with the flour, salt, and nuts. With your fingers, blend in the butter until the mixture is crumbly. Spread it over the apples, pressing it down.

6. Bake for 40 minutes, then turn up the oven to 400°F for 20 minutes longer, until the crumble is browned and bubbly and the apples are tender. Let cool on a rack. Serve warm or at room temperature.

7. Soften the ice cream. Stir in the Frangelico. Serve as a thick sauce with the crumble.

"Comfort me with apples for I am sick of love."
SONG OF SOLOMON

ALMOND APRICOT MERINGUE

★★ This dessert is for texture fanatics: crumbly meringue, chewy apricots, crunchy cookies, fluffy whipped cream—it's a rhapsody of oral impressions. If you focus your attention on the rhapsody, your troubles will fade into obscurity.

Makes one 10-inch pie

3 egg whites, at room temperature
Pinch of salt
Pinch of cream of tartar
1 cup sugar
1 teaspoon almond extract
½ cup finely crushed amaretti cookies
1 cup ground blanched almonds
½ cup diced dried apricots
Whipped cream, flavored with amaretto if
    desired

1. Preheat the oven to 350°F. Butter and flour a 10-inch pie pan.

2. Beat the egg whites with salt on low speed. When they get foamy, add cream of tartar and increase the beating speed. Beat until the whites hold soft peaks. Beat in the sugar, a tablespoon or so at a time. When half the sugar has been added, beat in the almond extract. Beat in the remaining sugar gradually. (Beat well between additions, and stop frequently to scrape down the sides with a rubber spatula.) The meringue is ready when it is glossy and stiff and no longer grainy from the sugar.

3. Fold in the crushed cookies, the almonds, and the apricots. Spread the mixture in the buttered pan. Bake for 30 minutes.

4. Let cool thoroughly on a rack. To serve, cut into wedges and top each with a dollop of whipped cream.

MAPLE CREAM

★★ If you are feeling melancholy, dose yourself with this exquisitely delicate mousse. Use pure maple syrup only.

Serves 6

1 envelope gelatin
1 cup milk
1 cup maple syrup
1 cup heavy cream, whipped

1. Soften the gelatin in ¼ cup cold water for 5 minutes.

2. Heat the milk in a deep heavy pan until it bubbles around the edges.

3. Stir the softened gelatin into the hot milk. Stir until it dissolves. Add the maple syrup and stir very well. Let cool until it is the consistency of unbeaten egg white.

4. When the mixture has cooled, force it through a sieve or fine strainer. Fold in the whipped cream.

5. Scrape the maple mixture into a glass bowl. Cover and chill for several hours.

TRIPLE CHOCOLATE BREAD PUDDING

✹✹✹ Bread pudding is supernal comfort food, and chocolate bread pudding is the ultimate of its kind. There is no doubt that this is an outrageous dessert. It is for those who want to wallow in chocolate. Use only the very best ingredients. I use Poulain cocoa, Hershey chocolate milk, and Tobler, Lindt, or Côte d'Or semisweet chocolate.

Serves 6–8

6 ounces stale French bread
8 tablespoons melted butter (1 stick)
1 cup coarsely chopped walnuts
8 ounces semisweet chocolate, chopped into
    ½-inch chunks
4 eggs
1 cup sugar
½ cup unsweetened cocoa, sifted

Pinch of salt
2 cups chocolate milk
½ teaspoon vanilla extract

1. Tear the bread into chunks approximately 1 inch square. Toss them in a bowl with the melted butter, walnuts, and chocolate chunks. Spread the mixture in a buttered 9 x 13 x 2-inch baking dish.

2. Beat the eggs lightly. Beat in the sugar, cocoa, salt, chocolate milk, and vanilla. Pour this mixture over the bread. Let it stand for at least ½ hour. With a broad spatula, occasionally push the bread down into the liquid as it soaks. Preheat the oven to 350°F.

3. Bake for 30 to 40 minutes, until the pudding is puffed and just set. Rush it to the table and serve *at once,* with softly whipped cream or slightly softened vanilla ice cream, if desired.

BAVARIAN APPLE CHEESECAKE

This dessert combines the best aspects of a cheesecake and apple pie. It was developed by Laurie Luntz for the Gourmetisseri in Atlanta.

Makes one 10-inch pie

6 large cooking apples
⅓ cup sugar
½ teaspoon cinnamon
⅓ cup butter
1 tablespoon oil
¾ teaspoon vanilla extract
⅓ cup sugar
Pinch of salt
1 cup flour
1 pound cream cheese at room temperature
½ cup sugar
2 eggs
1 tablespoon grated lemon peel
⅓ cup slivered almonds

1. Preheat the oven to 400°F.

2. Peel, core, and halve the apples. Cut them into ¼-inch wedges and place them in one layer in a baking dish. Cover the dish and bake for about 8 to 12 minutes, until the apples are soft but not mushy. Uncover the apples and set aside.

3. Blend the sugar and cinnamon in a small cup and set aside.

4. Blend the butter, oil, ¼ teaspoon vanilla, sugar, and salt. Blend in the flour. The dough will be crumbly. Pat the dough in a fairly thin layer on the bottom and halfway up the sides of a 9- or 10-inch springform pan.

5. Cream together the cheese and sugar. Beat in the remaining ingredients except the almonds and mix well.

6. Pour the cheese mixture into the crust and top with the warm apple slices. Sprinkle all of the cinnamon sugar on top of the apples and then sprinkle on the almonds.

7. Bake for 45 minutes to 1 hour. Run a knife around the edge of the pan while hot, let cool to room temperature on a rack, and then chill.

CHOCOLATE PATE

✹✹✹ Here is elegance for the chocoholic: thin slices of rich, dense, textured chocolate resting on crimson pools of thick raspberry sauce. It makes a stunning dessert for a dinner party, but it's even better as a solitary indulgence when you are badly in need of a culinary security blanket.

Serves 15

8 ounces semisweet chocolate
2 tablespoons unsweetened cocoa
6 tablespoons brandy
½ pound (2 sticks) butter, softened
2 tablespoons superfine sugar
2 eggs, separated
1 cup tightly packed ground blanched
     almonds (about 6 ounces)
Pinch of salt
Pinch of cream of tartar
Raspberry Sauce (recipe follows)

1. Line a 8½ x 4½ x 2½-inch loaf pan crosswise with two long sheets of wax paper. Lightly oil the paper with a tasteless vegetable oil. Set aside.

2. In a heavy saucepan, melt the chocolate with the cocoa and brandy over very low heat, stirring occasionally. When melted and perfectly smooth, set it aside to cool.

3. In an electric mixer, preferably with a paddle attachment, cream the butter. Beat in the sugar, then the yolks, one at a time. Incorporate them very well. Beat in the ground almonds and the cooled chocolate. Scrape the mixture into a large bowl.

4. In a clean bowl, beat the egg whites with salt until foamy. Add the cream of tartar and beat the whites until they hold firm peaks. Do not overbeat. With a rubber spatula quickly fold the whites into the chocolate mixture.

5. Pour and scrape the mixture into the prepared loaf pan. Rap it several times against the counter to eliminate air bubbles. Smooth the top. Fold the wax paper overhang over to cover, and refrigerate for at least a day. (It will keep in the refrigerator for at least a week.) To serve, uncover, invert the loaf pan over an attractive platter, and let the pâté slide out. Peel off the paper. Pour a puddle of raspberry sauce onto a dessert plate. With a sharp knife, cut a thin slice of pâté and place it on the sauce. Keep leftover pâté, well wrapped in plastic wrap, in the refrigerator.

Raspberry Sauce
Makes about 2½ cups

4 packages (10 ounces each) frozen
     raspberries in syrup, thawed
Sugar to taste (2–3 tablespoons)
1 tablespoon brandy

1. Drain the berries well. Purée in a food processor or blender. Force through a fine sieve or strainer into a bowl. Discard the seeds.

2. Stir in the sugar. This sauce must remain somewhat tart to be at its best, so taste as you add the sugar.

3. Stir in the brandy. Pour the sauce into a clear glass pitcher and refrigerate until serving time.

FROZEN BANANAS WITH PEANUT BUTTER FUDGE SAUCE

✱ If you really want to throw caution to the winds and have a thoroughly sybaritic and indulgent dessert, serve the bananas and sauce on ice cream, and top the whole thing with a blob of whipped cream.

Serves 6

3 large bananas, halved lengthwise
Peanut Butter Fudge Sauce (recipe follows)
Chopped salted peanuts

1. Wrap each banana half tightly in plastic wrap. Leave in the freezer for several hours.

2. Place frozen banana halves, cut side down, on cold dessert plates. Pour a generous amount of hot peanut butter fudge sauce over each half. Sprinkle with chopped peanuts and serve at once.

Peanut Butter Fudge Sauce
Makes about 1½ cups

¾ cup heavy cream
8 ounces peanut butter chips
3 ounces semisweet chocolate, chopped
1 tablespoon Frangelico

1. Bring cream to a boil in a saucepan.

2. Remove from heat. Stir in the peanut butter chips and the chocolate. Stir until perfectly smooth and melted. Stir in the Frangelico.

3. Store the sauce in the refrigerator in a tightly covered wide-mouthed container. At serving time, place the container in a bowl of hot water until the hardened mixture softens. Scrape it into a heavy saucepan and heat very, very gently, stirring occasionally.

CHOCOLATE CHUNK MACADAMIA MERINGUE COOKIES

✖✖✖ When all else fails, try chocolate chip cookies. A good one can raise the lowest spirits. Don't attempt this recipe on humid days—the cookies will not dry properly in the oven.

Makes about 2½ dozen

3 egg whites at room temperature
Pinch of salt
Pinch of cream of tartar
1 cup sugar
1 teaspoon vanilla extract
6 ounces semisweet chocolate, chopped into
  ½-inch chunks
3½ ounces macadamia nuts, very coarsely
  chopped

1. Preheat the oven to 375°F. Line two cookie sheets with baking parchment.

2. Beat the egg whites at low speed with salt until they begin to get foamy. Add cream of tartar, increase the beating speed, and beat until the whites hold soft peaks.

3. Beat in the sugar, a tablespoon or so at a time, stopping frequently to scrape down the sides of the bowl. When half the sugar has been added, beat in the vanilla. Beat in the remaining sugar a little at a time. The egg whites are ready when they are stiff and glossy and no longer grainy.

4. With a rubber spatula, fold the chocolate and nuts into the meringue. Drop the meringue mixture by the teaspoonful onto the parchment-lined sheets, leaving about 1½ inches of space between them. Bake for 20 minutes, turn off the oven, and leave in the closed oven for an additional hour. Remove from the oven and let sit on the cookie sheets for a few minutes. Then, with a metal spatula, remove the cookies to a rack to cool thoroughly. Store in a covered container.

"I cannot remember when I first ate a macadamia, but I was hooked... They were beautiful—so lumpy, Macadamian, salty, golden! I can still sense its complete Macadamianimity."
  M. F. K. FISHER
  With Bold Knife and Fork

82

COOKIES

A cookie is one of the friendliest objects in the world. A whole package of cookies is even friendlier. The supermarket cookie aisle is the repository for an astonishing array of palliatives. Who has not, in an hour of need, succumbed to the intense siren call of the Oreo, the Mallomar, or the Fig Newton? Is there anyone who has not, at one time or another, treated a depression with a Milano cookie, a chocolate-covered graham cracker, or a sugar wafer? A table set with a jelly glass of milk (with the carton standing by for refills), a brand-new unopened package of your favorite cookie, and a pile of paper napkins is better than a nap, a warm bubble bath, or a Marx Brothers' movie. As important as choosing the best cookie for your mood is the art of eating the cookie properly. As a helpful guide, here are a few examples of cookie technique:

Mallomar: With your teeth, scrape off the chocolate that covers the dome and eat it. Loosen the marshmallow dome from the bottom cookie base. Flip the dome into your mouth and with your tongue press it up against the roof of your mouth. (It feels wonderful.) Swallow it. Dunk the cookie base in milk and eat it.

Oreo: Gently life off the top of the cookie, being careful to leave all of the filling on the bottom half. Eat the top half, dunking or not, as you please. Place the bottom half against your teeth and scrape the white filling into your mouth (much like eating an artichoke leaf). Eat the bottom half.

Chocolate-covered graham cracker: Take a bite from the lower corner of the cookie and eat it. Dunk the cookie in the glass of milk. Hold it in the milk for a few moments—long enough for the cookie to soak up milk but not long enough for it to disintegrate. Pull out the cookie and eat it in several delicate bites. The graham cracker will be a milk-soaked sponge contained in a brittle chocolate crust. Exquisite!

Milano: Often these sandwich cookies are lopsided; the top and bottom are askew and the chocolate filling sticks out and forms a rim. Carefully nibble the chocolate rim all around the cookie. Only then can you finish the cookie in three or four bites. My son advises, "Milano cookies make a good side dish with homework."

Fig Newton: Eat it in small bites, alternating with sips of milk. Anything else is sacrilege.

CRANBERRY CRUNCH

✖✖✖ This is another American classic. The contrast of crunchy, sweet sugar, tart berries, and lightly spiced cake topping is very satisfying. Have a piece with a glass of milk when life seems dreary. Your outlook will immediately brighten.

Serves 6

4 cups (1 pound) cranberries, washed and
    picked over
1 orange
½ cup coarsely chopped walnuts
1¾ cups sugar
2 eggs

⅛ teaspoon ground allspice
⅛ teaspoon ground cinnamon
⅛ teaspoon grated nutmeg
1 cup flour
8 tablespoons (1 stick) butter, melted and
    cooled
½ teaspoon orange extract
Vanilla ice cream, slightly softened and
    mixed with a bit of orange liqueur if
    desired

1. Preheat the oven to 350°F.

2. Butter a 10-inch round shallow baking
dish or pie pan.

3. Put the cranberries in a bowl. With a cit-

rus zester, grate the orange rind over the
bowl (so that the rind and some of the orange
oil go into the bowl). Toss in the walnuts and
¾ cup sugar. Spread the mixture in the buttered dish.

4. Beat the eggs. Beat in the seasonings and
the remaining sugar. Stir in the flour. Gradually beat in the melted butter and orange
extract.

5. Pour and spread the batter over the cranberries. Don't worry if it doesn't quite spread
to the edges. Bake for 40 to 45 minutes, until
the topping is set.

6. Let cool on a rack for about ½ hour. Serve
warm with softened ice cream.

BUTTERMILK APRICOT-SPICE CAKE

✸✸ This is an old-fashioned
farmhouse-type spice cake, laced
with chunks of dried apricots. It has
a wonderfully moist texture. I love
this cake made with prunes, but to
my surprise, many people hate them
and actually pick them out of the
cake. If you find comfort in the rich
taste and texture of prunes, substitute them for the apricots.

Makes one 9 x 13-inch cake

2 cups self-rising flour
1 teaspoon allspice
¼ teaspoon ground cloves
1 teaspoon grated nutmeg
1 teaspoon ground cinnamon
3 eggs
1½ cups sugar
1 cup buttermilk
1 cup vegetable oil
1½ cups coarsely chopped dried apricots,
    simmered in water to cover until tender,
    and drained
Icing (see facing page)

84

1. Preheat the oven to 350°F.

2. Sift the flour and spices into a bowl. Set aside.

3. Beat the eggs well. Gradually add sugar, beating well.

4. Gradually add buttermilk and oil, beating well all the while.

5. Stir in the flour-spice mixture until well blended.

6. Fold in the drained chopped apricots.

7. Pour into a well-greased 9 x 13-inch baking pan. Bake for 45 minutes, or until done. (The cake will pull away from the sides of the pan, and it will spring back when lightly pressed.)

8. While cake is still hot from the oven, gently poke it in several places with a fork and pour the icing over it. Let cool.

9. Serve in squares, right from the baking pan.

Icing

1 cup sugar
½ cup buttermilk
1 tablespoon butter
1 teaspoon vanilla extract
1 teaspoon baking soda

1. Combine all ingredients in a heavy deep nonreactive saucepan. Bring to a boil and boil, stirring, for 2 minutes.

2. Immediately pour the hot mixture over the cake, distributing it as evenly as possible. The icing will sink in, creating a lovely moist texture.

BITTERSWEET CHOCOLATE SAUCE FOR ICE CREAM

Makes approximately 1 ¼ cups

3 bittersweet Toblerone bars (3 ounces each)
½ cup heavy cream
1–2 tablespoons kirsch

1. Break up chocolate bars and combine in a heavy saucepan with the cream and kirsch.

2. Heat gently, stirring occasionally, until melted, smooth, and hot.

NOTE This will keep refrigerated for weeks. Store in a wide-mouthed container. At serving time, place the container in a bowl of hot water until the hardened mixture softens. Scrape into a double boiler or heavy saucepan. Heat gently and serve.

INSTANT RASPBERRY ICE CREAM

✻This quick and easy, vividly flavored ice cream is a low-cal comfort, but if you want to be devilishly unconcerned with calories, serve each scoop in a puddle of heavy cream. If the only frozen raspberries in syrup you can find are in "lite syrup," sprinkle each scoop with a bit of dark brown sugar.

Makes 2½ cups

2 packages (10 ounces each) frozen
    raspberries in syrup
⅔ cup very cold buttermilk
1 teaspoon orange extract

1. Remove the berries from the freezer and leave out for 10 minutes. Use a sharp knife to cut the frozen fruit into chunks. Put the chunks in a food processor bowl with the buttermilk and orange extract.

2. Process until the fruit is puréed and the mixture is of a thick ice cream-like consistency. Stop to scrape down the sides of the bowl occasionally. Scoop into dessert goblets and serve at once.

COLD COMFORT

For instant solace, nothing beats ice cream. It's cheaper than a psychiatrist, safer than whiskey, and almost foolproof. What depression remains unlifted when the vanilla is filled with crunchy chunks of Oreo, the chocolate bristles with chocolate chips, and the butter pecan is rich and well nutted? The good news is that ice cream for grownups is in. It is perfectly acceptable, even chic, to publicly indulge in this most satisfying of culinary therapies.

The very best way to indulge in ice cream is to dive into a sundae. In the early twentieth century, soda water was a Sunday no-no. Soda fountain proprietors, eager to satisfy Sunday customers blue laws or no, invented the special Sunday-only ice cream soda, without the soda—the sundae. (The "y" was changed to "e" so that the name of the sabbath would not be taken in vain.) Sundaes, made with scoops of high-quality ice cream, blanketed with heavenly rich sauces and topped with generous dollops of freshly whipped cream, make the most ravishing dessert imaginable. Hot sauces on ice cream, of course, make the classic and irresistible "hot as summer, cold as winter" effect, but a cold sauce (see Raspberry Sauce, page 80) can be pretty spectacular, too. Serve an ice cream buffet of the best ice creams you can buy, clouds of whipped cream, and several homemade sauces. Don't forget Peanut Butter Fudge Sauce (page 81).

BUTTERSCOTCH SAUCE FOR ICE CREAM

✳✳

Makes approximately 1 ¾ cups

8 tablespoons (1 stick) butter
1 cup firmly packed dark brown sugar
½ cup buttermilk

Melt the butter. Stir in the sugar. Stir in the buttermilk. Bring to a boil, stirring. Boil until the mixture reaches 220°F on a candy thermometer. Let cool. Store in the refrigerator. Serve at room temperature.

SINLESS CHOCOLATE MOUSSE

✳✳ When you've just *got* to have some chocolate to brighten a gloomy day, but you are also desperately trying to keep the calories at bay, take heart! This mousse is rich and chocolaty, yet at least 100 calories less per serving than the usual chocolate mousse.

Serves 8

6 ounces semisweet chocolate, coarsely
    chopped
6 packets Equal (Aspartame)
2 tablespoons hot strong coffee
2 eggs
2 egg yolks
¾ cup evaporated skim milk, heated
1 ½ tablespoons dark rum

1. Put the chocolate, Equal, coffee, eggs, and egg yolks in the container of a blender or food processor, in the order given.

2. Turn the machine on and immediately pour in the hot milk in a steady stream. Add rum. Continue blending or processing for 1 minute. Pour into 8 dessert glasses or goblets. Cover well and chill in the freezer for 2 to 3 hours until firmly set.

"The greatest tragedies were written by the Greeks and by Shakespeare. Neither knew chocolate. The Swiss are known for nonviolence. They are also known for superb chocolate."
SANDRA BOYNTON
Chocolate: The Consuming Passion

BLACK AND WHITE CHOCOLATE PIE

✳✳✳ This chocolate lover's fantasy features a hard, nut-studded white chocolate crust filled with a creamy, fluffy dark chocolate mousse. It's very easy to make and intensely pleasurable to eat.

Makes one 9-inch pie

6 ounces white chocolate (Tobler Narcisse)
2 tablespoons butter
1 cup finely chopped walnuts
6 ounces semisweet chocolate, in pieces
2 tablespoons sugar
1 tablespoon hot strong coffee
1 egg
1 egg yolk
½ cup heavy cream, scalded
2 tablespoons dark rum
½ cup heavy cream, whipped
Additional white chocolate for garnish

1. Line a 9-inch pie plate with foil. Butter lightly.

2. Melt the white chocolate with the butter in a heavy saucepan over low heat. Stir in the nuts.

3. Pour and scrape the mixture into the foil-lined plate. Use a rubber spatula to spread the mixture evenly on the bottom and up the sides of the plate. Refrigerate for 2 to 3 hours, until firm.

4. When thoroughly set, remove the chocolate shell from the pie plate and gently peel off the foil. Set the shell back in the pie plate and return it to the refrigerator while you make the dark chocolate filling.

5. Place the semisweet chocolate, sugar, hot coffee, egg, and yolk in the container of a food processor or blender in the order given. Turn on the machine and immediately pour in the hot cream in a steady stream. Add the rum. Process or blend for 1 minute. Pour the mixture into a bowl and let cool slightly.

6. Fold the whipped cream into the chocolate mixture. Spoon it into the white chocolate shell. Cover with plastic wrap and refrigerate for several hours, until the chocolate filling is set.

7. At serving time, carefully tip the pie out of the pie pan and set it on a flat plate. With a vegetable peeler, shave chocolate curls from a bar of white chocolate. Heap the chocolate curls in the center of the pie. Serve.

GINGER LIME MOUSSE

✳✳You will want to eat this dessert very slowly, savoring each smooth, subtle mouthful. The ginger-lime-buttermilk combination is remarkably good.

Serves 6

2 cups heavy cream
2 heaping tablespoons freshly grated ginger
    root
Grated zest of ½ lime
1½ envelopes gelatin
Juice of 1 lime
½ cup sugar
2 cups buttermilk

1. In a deep heavy pot, boil the cream with the ginger and lime zest until reduced by ½ cup.

2. Soften the gelatin in ½ cup cold water for 5 minutes.

3. Thoroughly stir the lime juice, gelatin, and sugar into the cream. Let cool to room temperature, stirring occasionally.

4. Strain the mixture through a fine sieve, pushing down on the solids to extract all their juices. Whisk in the buttermilk. Pour the mixture into a pretty glass serving bowl or into 6 individual glass dessert goblets. Chill for several hours, until set.

HALVAH MOUSSE

✳✳✳ If you don't know about halvah, rush out to the nearest Jewish deli or ethnic food emporium at once and buy a hefty piece of the dense Middle Eastern confection. It is made of honey and ground sesame seeds; sometimes studded with almonds or pistachios, marbled with swirls of chocolate flavor, or covered with hard chocolate. This mousse is a halvah-flecked cloud. Pure heaven for halvah freaks.

Serves 8

½ pound marble halvah with nuts
2 cups heavy cream
2 egg whites at room temperature
Pinch of salt
Pinch of cream of tartar
¼ cup sugar

1. Put the halvah on a wooden board. With a hand chopper, chop it into fine flakes.

2. Whip the cream until it holds soft peaks. (Do not overwhip, or the cream will release a quantity of moisture later, and your mousse will be soupy rather than fluffy.) Fold in the flaked halvah.

3. In a clean bowl, with a clean beater, beat the egg whites slowly. As they get foamy, add salt and cream of tartar and increase the beating speed. When the egg whites hold soft peaks, add the sugar, a tablespoon at a time. The egg whites are ready when they look like marshmallow cream and are no longer grainy from the sugar.

4. Fold the whites gently but thoroughly into the halvah cream mixture. Scrape into a pretty serving bowl, smooth the top, and cover with plastic wrap. Refrigerate overnight.

EASY HALVAH ICE CREAM ✳✳

If you're hankering for an indulgently creamy and delicious halvah dessert, but have neither the time nor the inclination to make the mousse, take a pint of very good vanilla ice cream out of the freezer to soften for a few minutes. Put a 4-ounce bar of chocolate-covered halvah on a wooden chopping board. Chop it into coarse flakes (it should not be as finely chopped as for the mousse). Scrape the ice cream into a bowl. Fold the chopped halvah and chocolate thoroughly into the ice cream. Pack the ice cream back into its container. Return to the freezer. It can stay there for weeks, but of course it won't last that long. Let it resoften for a few minutes before serving.

BROWNIE PIE WITH WHITE CHOCOLATE CHUNKS

✹✹Classic brownies—sweet and fudgy—get a lift from bits of white chocolate. The mixture is baked in a round dish and cut into wedges like a pie.

Makes one 9-inch pie

8 tablespoons (1 stick) butter, softened
1 cup sugar
2 eggs
½ cup flour
¼ cup unsweetened cocoa, sifted
1 teaspoon vanilla extract
½ cup coarsely chopped walnuts or pecans
3 ounces white chocolate, broken into ½-inch pieces

1. Preheat the oven to 325°F.

2. Cream the butter with the sugar. Beat in the eggs. Stir in the flour, cocoa, and vanilla. Fold in the nuts and white chocolate. Pour and scrape the batter into a greased 9-inch pie pan.

3. Bake for approximately 35 minutes. A cake tester will test not quite clean. This pie should be moist. Let cool on a rack. This is good when slightly warm, or when thoroughly cooled. When cool, keep well covered.

NURSERY FOOD

When life is cruel, when fortune frowns and the cares of the world lie heavy on the soul, turn to nursery food. It is the most felicitous of all comfort foods. Sit home all alone with a dish of rice pudding, a plate of macaroni and cheese, or a bowl of mashed potatoes, and water each spoonful with your tears. Chances are, by the time the plate or bowl is scraped clean, your tears will be gone and your anxiety will be lulled into serenity. For serious sorrows, the nursery food must be completely bland. Don't fool around with fancy ingredients. A pepper mill must never come near the potatoes, candied ginger or raisins soaked in rum have no business lurking in the rice pudding, and strong, smelly cheeses must never mar the macaroni and cheese. Nursery food must remain bland, soothing, and innocent if its magic is to work.

"Sometimes all I want is food that makes me feel warm and content. I hunger not for the vanilla bean pasta that shows the chef's imagination but for the rice pudding that comes from his heart."

CAROLINE BATES
Gourmet magazine

MRS. GROSSO'S RICOTTA CHEESECAKE

✷✷ Italian-style cheesecakes made with ricotta cheese have great delicacy. This one is particularly easy to make because everything is mixed together in one bowl. As it bakes, it forms its own crust.

Makes one 9-inch cake

2 packages (8 ounces each) cream cheese
1 pound ricotta cheese
1 pint sour cream
1½ cups sugar
4 eggs
5 teaspoons vanilla extract
5 teaspoons lemon juice
3 tablespoons flour
3 tablespoons cornstarch

1. Preheat the oven to 350°F.

2. Beat together the cream cheese, ricotta cheese, and sour cream. Beat in the sugar. Beat in the remaining ingredients, one at a time. Everything must be very well combined.

3. Pour the mixture into a greased 9-inch springform pan. Bake for 1 hour. Turn off the oven (do not open the oven door) and leave the cake in the oven for 1 hour longer.

4. Let the cake cool on a rack, then refrigerate overnight. The next day, remove the sides of the springform pan, cut the cake, and serve.

NOTE Occasionally this cake will emerge from the oven with a crack on top. Don't worry, it will still be delicious.

PEANUT BUTTER MOUSSE

✷✷✷ For peanut butter fans and dessert lovers, this mousse is almost too good to be true. Feed it to your melancholy friends; watch them gasp and close their eyes in ecstasy.

Serves 10

2 cups smooth peanut butter
1 pound ricotta cheese, at room temperature
2 cups confectioners' sugar
2½ tablespoons heavy cream
1 tablespoon vanilla extract
2 cups heavy cream, whipped
Grated bittersweet chocolate

1. Cream together the peanut butter and the ricotta cheese. Beat in the sugar. Beat in the cream and vanilla. The mixture must be very smooth and well combined.

2. Fold the whipped cream into the peanut butter mixture. Spoon the mixture into individual glass globlets. Chill for several hours.

Garnish with grated chocolate just before serving.

VARIATION Spoon a puddle of warm Chocolate Sauce (see page 85) onto each dessert plate. With a small ice cream scoop, scoop out 2 to 3 scoops of mousse and place them on the sauce. Omit the grated chocolate.

RICE PUDDING

✖✖✖ When the Rice Council sponsored a rice pudding contest, recipes came pouring in from all sorts of restaurants, featuring decidedly un-rice-pudding-like ingredients: pears and blackberries, grenadine and coconut, kiwi fruit and mangoes. Interesting as hell, but no use whatsoever for a blue funk. Thank goodness for the Coach House in New York City. Their rice pudding is pure innocence, and will lull you into blissful calm.

Serves 8–10

7 cups milk
¾ cup uncooked long-grain rice
    (unconverted)
¾ cup sugar
5 eggs
1 cup heavy cream

1 teaspoon vanilla extract
Ground cinnamon

1. Rinse a deep heavy pot with cold water. Do not dry it. Bring the milk to a boil in the pot. Stir in the rice and sugar. Reduce the heat to medium and simmer for about 35 minutes, stirring frequently, until the rice is very tender and the mixture is very thick. Do not let it scorch. Remove from heat.

2. Beat the eggs in a mixing bowl until they are frothy. Stir in the cream. Slowly dribble 2 cups of the hot rice mixture into the eggs, beating continuously.

3. Stir the egg mixture into the remaining rice. Return to the stove and cook over medium heat for 5 minutes, or until the mixture coats a spoon. Stir in the vanilla.

4. Pour the pudding into a large shallow dish. Sprinkle with cinnamon. Chill. To serve, spoon into pretty goblets.

Index